Clear the Tracks!

JOSEPH BROMLEY

CLEAR THE TRACKS!

THE STORY OF AN OLD-TIME LOCOMOTIVE ENGINEER

AS TOLD TO PAGE COOPER

ILLUSTRATED BY STEPHEN J. VOORHIES

WHITTLESEY HOUSE

New York   MCGRAW-HILL BOOK COMPANY, INC.   *London*

A PATHFINDER BOOK REPRINT EDITION
Complete and Unabridged

Printed in the United States of America

ISBN: 979-8869109378

PUBLISHED BY WHITTLESEY HOUSE
A division of the McGraw-Hill Book Company, Inc.

I have tried to recapture the old days on the Lackawanna in memory of the veterans who were my heroes when I first began to ride the engines: Tom Thatcher, the "Old Man," whose accusing glass eye struck terror to the very marrow of my bones; A. C. Salsbury, the "Supe"; John Teller, William Reese, Nick Kuhn, Billy Worrell, Fred Willkie, John Keach, James Watson, Pat Grace, John Yeoman, Tracy Shaw, Frank Quinn—conductors and engineers on the Utica Division. They have long since made their last run west, but they live in the memory of many an old-timer who learned his job in those grand, prodigious days of the railroads.

Contents

1. The Old Black River Line

As long as I can remember, railroading has been in my blood. The first sounds that registered on my ears were the whistles of the New York Central trains hooting for a crossing. They drifted over the hill to the farm, calling me to follow the iron pike. When I was old and sturdy enough to walk six miles to the railroad, I sat on an embankment above the tracks and watched the trains go by, waved to the lordly creatures leaning out of the cab windows, with the wind parting their whiskers, and made up my mind that I too was going to run one of those snorting engines with red-and-yellow wheels and their names in gold letters on their sides.

Actually I began railroading at sixteen as a "callboy" in the yards of the old Black River Line in Utica; but the date that stands out in my memory as the beginning of the scramble up the ladder was the night that I first called old Phil Doubleday, the tough, lazy, cantankerous old-timer who made me an engineer.

It was dark by six o'clock on that December evening in 1880. On the way to work I had passed the lamplighter with his blowtorch putting a flame to the benzene lamps.

In the yard I remember how sleek and black the rails looked, making patterns on the roadbed sprinkled with snow, and how clear the bunches of switch lights glowed, red and green, like baubles that had fallen from a Christmas tree. The switchmen on the night "trick" were leaving the yard office shack. I could see the red belly of the stove glowing through the open door; and already a couple of yard engines, old demoted "goats," were at work, their wheels screeching on the wet rails as they reached into a jumble of switches, pulled out strings of freight cars and kicked them onto other tracks.

Through the window of the Master Mechanic's office I saw that John Bailey had finished copying the call list from the blackboard on the wall behind his desk; so I went in and held out my fingers to the stove. His office was a corner of the shop, and as I waited while he checked the list (pausing to smooth his long white beard, waved as carefully as a woman's hair), I could see behind him the shadows of engine parts lying about the floor: a couple of wheels, which caught the light of his swinging lamp, the hulk of a dismounted cab and the gleam of a brass engine-bell turned over on its side. John was proud of his beard and could not keep his hands off it, so I stood on one foot then the other while he punctuated his orders with caressing strokes.

"Here you are, Joe. The only thing you've got to watch out for is Doubleday. I want him to run the 'roustabout' that's marked up for 2:31. Call him about a quarter of two and stick around to see that he doesn't break his neck coming across the dump. One of these nights his bones are going to fall apart, but he'll keep on running as long as he can climb into a cab. In his day he had one of the lightest hands on the throttle you ever saw, could pull out a 'passenger' as gently as if it were a baby carriage."

John walked over to the board and consulted the names posted on the "extra" column.

"Call Sugarfoot Frank to fire, or if you can't find him, Dixie Burns."

The old man sighed as he folded the call sheet. He was probably little over sixty but to me he looked as hoary as a prophet. "When I first went firing, all a caller had to do was to stick his head in John Collins' saloon over on Water Street and shout 'Wood up!' and every one of us who was able, would make for the door. But not any more. Rule G has made us a bunch of suds-wipers, Joe. There aren't many of the hollow-legs left who could fill up with whiskey straight and make a record run to Watertown."

Heaving his great bulk into his pivot chair, the Master Mechanic gave me the list and waved me away. I went outside, where the lanterns of the brakemen were swinging red arcs in the dusk. The yardmaster was cursing a pin-puller who had missed a jump for the stirrup of a boxcar and sprained his wrist, and as I listened, my pride nearly burst the buttons of my leather jacket: I was a railroad man.

For two months I had been callboy; already I was dreaming that John Bailey would let me go out on an engine as a student fireman, a "tallow pot," next spring, and then it would be no time until I was set up with an engine of my own, pulling freight over the hump of the

Adirondacks and down into the valley of the St. Lawrence —following the river that cut rock gorges and snaked its tortuous, black way through forests toward Ogdensburg on the Canadian border, or hauling the timber from the sawmills of Watertown. And one day I would be on the best run of them all, a fast passenger carrying summer people to Cape Vincent and the Thousand Islands.

To hang out of the right-hand window of the cab of a through train and whistle an arrogant toot to the girls at the crossings then seemed to me a gallant adventure, and after sixty years the feel of the throttle under my hand and the shriek of the whistle still warm my blood. But we can't toot to the girls any more. Life is regulated: so many toots at a way station, so many long and so many short at a crossing. The "Book of Rules" took a lot of carefree individualism out of railroading.

But in the old days, when a train highballed out of the station, the engineer was on his own, a man who rode destiny and twisted her tail. To be sure, the fingers of the old brass-pounders were stretching out after him, trying to harness him to telegraph keys; but on the old Black River Line most of the operators didn't work after five o'clock, and they weren't too scrupulous about the time they reported you out of sight. Sometimes they were almost human and understood that a smoke-maker and his "brains," as we ironically called the conductor, liked to go fishing.

But I have wandered from that frosty December night when I set out to call old Phil Doubleday and got a toe hold in the industry which more than any other of her mighty enterprises has united the people of America. Although I was inarticulate, and compressed into the one word "railroading" all this sense of the mystery of far places and peoples and the things they lived by, it was the glamor of them that held me in the roundhouse to watch Black River Jack bring in Number 17, the fast afternoon passenger from Ogdensburg.

He was one of the "big four," the quartette of engineers who were the royalty of the line, and I looked with awe at his bold, leathery face trimmed with a black mustache that stuck out at right angles like the arms of a weather vane. He had already backed the engine into the turntable and was climbing out of the cab. The brakemen streaked past me toward the yardmaster's office to turn in their signal lamps and flags, and a goat was already pulling the coaches into the yard.

"Hi, Nobby!" Jack waved to me and hurried over to sign off. He called me by the nickname that the men in the shop gave me because I wore white celluloid collars that mother had bought for me when I got the job, and I was so proud I wouldn't have called the king my uncle.

Crossing the tracks I started my round on the town side, where the engineers and conductors of the highball trains lived in pretty little houses with front yards and gardens. This was the "right" side of the tracks. After two months I could find any of their doors in a blind fog. First was "Hiki's" house—he was Bill Williams, and "Mister" to his face, for he was a proud man, another of the princely four. He neither drank nor cursed, but when he shouted his private swear word "hiki!" the thunder of his voice could bounce a string of coal cars off the track. Hiki was eating his supper in the kitchen.

"Number 6 at 7:35," I shouted through the kitchen door. It was a routine call. Six days a week he took out the fast passenger with the coaches from New York and brought Number 5 back from Watertown.

"All right, Nobby. Come and have a cup of coffee." His wife offered me a fat piece of layer cake with chocolate icing, and I ate decorously, watching Hiki maneuver his oversized mustache cup. Then on to call the conductors and Baldy and Rubberguts.

Baldy came to the door in his undershirt—a big, handsome man, the image of Buffalo Bill except for his naked skull. He had been a captain on the Great Lakes, and I could see the tattooing on his arms: women in tights and in nothing at all; American flags, eagles, stars.

"Thank you, Nobby," he said. "Won't you come in and get warm?" But I shook my head, embarrassed by his imposing dignity.

For the other calls I crossed the yards to railroad town, weaving through the unhooked cars of the fast freight that had just pulled in. The goats were clawing at her, one at each end, breaking her up, cutting out the cars of perishables and shifting them to the outer edge of the yard, where they would be unloaded and hauled to the freight house before the market opened.

From behind the green light at the end of a switching track a "cut" of cars rolled down on me, enormous in the dark. The "brakie" on top stood with his club in the wheel, ready to throw the brake. As I jumped to one side, he gave it a twist, the cars slowed down and the front one eased to a stop not more than two feet from the light. Leaning over the roof the "shack" laughed at me.

"Don't be afraid, kid. It's not a runaway."

Around one o'clock when the streets were deserted, except for the lanterns of two or three lone railroaders coming home from a late train, I went to call Old Phil, who lived in a little cottage set by itself on the further edge of the city dump. Playing my flashlight on the narrow path along the edge, I tried not to step on the huge rats that scurried across my feet and rattled the tin cans. Once a mound of cans started to roll, and I could hear it behind me, clattering like a landslide into the path.

The shack was a black huddle in a little open garden space, gray in the feeble light of a rising moon. The picket gate was open and I went in, but as I put my foot on the rickety stoop before the door, a dog began to bark.

"Down, Fly, down! Shut your loud mouth," ordered a cracked old voice. I pounded on the door, and in a few minutes Old Phil stuck out his head.

"Call to take out the roustabout at 2:31, Mr. Doubleday. I'll wait and walk back with you. It's sorta lonely going by the dump."

"All right, sonny, be with you in a minute."

"I could hear the murmur of a woman's voice inside and the shuffling of feet. Presently Old Phil came to the door with his lunch box in one hand and in the other a can of something that had the damp, earthy smell of fishing worms. He whistled to the dog, and the three of us went back along the path, I in the lead with the flashlight and the dog keeping to Old Phil's heels.

"Can you sing, my boy? A good song always frightens away the dump critters." Without waiting for an answer,

he began to shout with all his might the high, quavery saga of the dying engineer:

> "Oh, let me on that engine there.
> I'll make the old girl snort and rare,
> Oh, let me at some water tank
> Make a big-hole stop and give a yank!"

Fly began to howl softly and ran ahead, sniffing for rats.

> "Then from the corner of my eye
> I'll watch the pieces as they fly;
> Then I'll calmly, softly sit me down
> And watch the dust clouds settle round."

Back into the alleys we plunged, narrow canyons that threw his voice from wall to wall. A window opened and an angry voice yelled, "Shut up, you lousy bum. Can't you let a fellow sleep?" For answer, Phil stopped under the window and shouted:

> "Oh, just once more before I'm dead
> Let me stand the conductor on his head;
> Let me see him crawl from beneath the wreck
> With a window sash hung 'round his neck."

A beer bottle shot out of the window. It hit me a glancing blow on the head, bounced off and cracked to splinters on the street. My knees caved in, and for a moment everything went black. When I came to, Fly was licking my fingers and Old Phil trying to hold me up.

"By God, sonny, I'll blast that uncivilized varmint for knocking you down. Can you lean against the wall while I go in and paste him one?"

The strength was coming back to my knees, and through the fog in my mind there was only one insistent thought: I must get Old Phil to the enginehouse in time to take out the roustabout.

Putting out my hand, I leaned on his shoulder. "I'm dizzy," I said, "and I can't be late. Will you let me lean on you to the roundhouse?"

"Of course, my boy. It was all my fault. Come on.

Old Phil will take care of you." Carefully he led me across the tracks, saying, "Step up," and "Step down," and "Watch out for the iron." When he left me at the "ready" track, where the train was made up ready to go out, he climbed on his engine and threw down a bed of waste for Fly.

"You can count on Old Phil, chum," he called as he squirted a jet of steam from his cylinder cocks. I'll make it up to you, son. You see if I don't."

He pulled out, and I went and sat down on an oil tin in a corner of the enginehouse. Somehow I managed to stay around until six o'clock; but when I got home and mother put me to bed, there was a lump on my head as big as a walnut.

2. The Gravel Pit

VERY TIME HE SAW ME, OLD PHIL FUSSED about the bump on my head; but it soon went down, and I was too busy to worry about anything, for I was finding twenty-four hours a day hardly long enough to cram into my head all the fascinating sounds and smells and lingo of the railroad. My trick was from six o'clock in the evening until six in the morning, but by running home the minute I reported off duty, gobbling the hot breakfast that mother had waiting for me and promptly falling into bed, I was able to reach the yards again by three o'clock in the afternoon. John Bailey let me stay around the shops and the roundhouse, running errands for him and hunting up pieces of waste for the firemen who were polishing brass.

The roundhouse, which was the garage of the line's twenty-two high-stacked, wood-burning engines, was as murky as a pit in hell, and full of noise. Usually five or six engines were in—some of them just off the run, belching into the "smoke racks" over their heads (ventilators that stuck up through the roof and were supposed to carry off the smoke); others puffing a hot black breath as they got up steam. Above them hung a cloud of vapor that smelled of hot oil and steam and good, pungent burning wood. On the tracks that spidered out from the turntable, Baldy and Rubberguts and the runners of the freights puttered about with oil cans, tinkering with their buggies. The engineer all but owned the engine and made it a glorified reflection of his personality. He bought it handsome tallow pots, bells, and whistles, pasted pictures in the cab and adorned it according to his fancy. If Black River Jack wanted the high driving-wheels of his engine painted red or yellow or blue with white strips, he gave his fireman a can of paint; and sometimes he even sank a large hunk of his pay into real gold leaf for lettering on the cab.

When the engine was laid up for repairs, the engineer was laid off too; so he looked it over every time he came in off a run and tried to keep it out of the shops. Sometimes he trusted a fireman to grind a cylinder, but not often. His tallow pot was the engine's nursemaid; he kept her clean and polished the brass until it shone like gold. Sometimes a tallow pot let me wash down the jacket, but I was never allowed to touch the brass.

George Hughes, the fire boy, was my age; and we were each making ninety cents a day, so we were neck and neck in the business. His job was to fill an engine with wood when it was time to get up steam, and toss in a lighted piece of waste. The draft was so good in those old balloon stacks that he never needed kindling. He high-hatted me in the round-house, but on our afternoons off we hunted and skated together, or went skylarking with the gashouse gang. Irish Ed, the gang's chief, was the grandson of Phil Doubleday and a constant grief to the old fellow—not because he was a tough, mischievous kid, always getting into trouble, but because he worked for the gas company instead of the railroad. But the old lady had a soft spot for him; and when we went over to the neat little shack across the dump, she gave us doughnuts and we helped her gather wood or sweep the yard.

Old Phil was always ready to tell me stories or show me how he trained Fly and Pete, the robin that lived in a birdhouse under the roof. Pete did a lot of chattering, and knew how to ask for his dinner by ringing a bell—clinging to a ribbon that was tied to the clapper and swinging back and forth, playing an impatient tune until the old man came out with a handful of bread and crumbs and dried sunflower seed.

One day in March when Old Phil took Fly and me frog hunting, he told me that John Bailey was sending him out in April with a gravel train and that he was going to run "the Butterfly."

"Getting a regular run, Nobby, a regular run. When you look for me on the call board, you won't find me in the 'extra' list."

The gravel pit was only two miles away; but Old Phil threw back his shoulders as if he were taking out the fast freight to Ogdensburg. He almost made my eyes leak, for everyone knew that he was the last engineer John Bailey called. He wouldn't get much of a fireman, no one who would take an interest in the Butterfly. The next afternoon I went over to the old engine—Number 1 she was, the oldest on the road—and dusted off her cobwebs. Dirt and ashes covered her like a thick coat of paint, but when

I had washed and greased her cab, *Theodore Butterfield* stood out in high gold letters. She had been named for one of the stockholders of the road, the man who owned the Butterfield House, the Waldorf of Utica; but to the men in the yard she was always "the Butterfly."

Every day I worked on the engine, shined her brass trimmings and polished her handsome bell until John Bailey could have curled his beard in it. I swept the cab, sewed in the leaky stuffings in the engineer's cushion with a piece of twine and, when no one was looking, climbed into the cab and made believe I was running her, pushing the lever and opening up the throttle.

One afternoon when I was painting her tall balloon stack, which bulged out at the top like a potato on a stick, Irish Ed came running into the roundhouse as if the devil were snapping at his heels. He looked around for George, who was wooding up Number 13, whispered to him and in a moment they both came over to the Butterfly, circling around behind her on the side next the wall.

"Look here, Joe," George Hughes said out of the side of his mouth (although nobody else could hear him for the clatter of Number 18 rolling onto the turntable). "Ed has pretty near killed a man. The fellow's in the hospital. We've got to hide him in the Butterfly."

We looked around. Hiki's tallow pot was touching up the yellow spokes of his wheels, an engineer over by the doors was looking at his bushings, and Baldy, the dandy—immaculate in fresh overalls and a starched white shirt with the sleeves folded neatly back to the elbows—was taking out Number 22. Nobody was paying the slightest attention to us, so we hoisted Ed into the tank of the Butterfly and covered him with some pieces of burlap.

That night when I was calling, I brought him water and one of my sandwiches; and when I went across the tracks to knock up a couple of shacks for an extra freight, I went by Phil's house and told him that Ed had got into a fight. The old lady wrung her hands and cried; but Phil walked across the dump with me and asked if we could keep that dratted, half-baked noodle-puncher hidden until the next night. No one, he said, would think of looking for him in the Butterfly.

George came early in the morning, swung his lunch box under my nose and gave me a look that said he was prepared for anything. When I got home, I was too excited to sleep; so I started back early in the afternoon and found George talking to a cop, the one who used to chase us out of the sand lot. With my heart pounding in my throat I grabbed a handful of waste and began to polish the nearest engine, standing with my back to them but stretching my ears to hear George swear he hadn't seen Ed for a couple of days.

That night around two o'clock I met Old Phil at the roundhouse and stood guard at the doors while he yanked Ed out of the Butterfly, took him into the yard and boosted him into a boxcar that was going out empty on a "wildcat," a train that did not run on schedule. It was made up on a near track, and I could see everything as in a shadow show. The flagman dropped off the caboose and put his hand on the old man's shoulder, the switch at the entrance to the yard flashed the green "go ahead," the conductor swung the highball and climbed into the caboose and the wildcat pulled out. It was the last I ever saw of Ed.

From that night on Old Phil kept telling me that I was the only boy he had and kept prodding me to get ahead. He wanted me to fire the Butterfly and was after me to ask John Bailey for the job, until one evening I got up the courage and spoke to "Moses" about it when he handed me the call list. The Master Mechanic screwed around in his pivot chair and stroked his beard while he looked me over.

"Sorry, Joe," he boomed, "but you're too light. I bet you don't weigh a hundred pounds."

He was right, but I couldn't give up so easily, not with Old Phil urging me to go to him again and grumbling that if I didn't get the job they would give it to some "damned Sunday School boy."

A day or two later I tried again, and this time John was a bit testy.

"Now, Nobby, you know very well you're too light and too young, but I'll think it over."

On the last day of March I told mother not to worry if I didn't come back in the morning, as I might be going out on the gravel train. Then I went down early and stood around where Bailey couldn't overlook me. When he gave me the call list, I saw that Old Phil was marked down to pull the gravel train; but Mr. Bailey said I needn't call a fireman, as Mr. Maynard, the Superintendent, was sending down somebody from his Sunday School class. So Old Phil hadn't been joking, after all!

Gnawing wormwood I made the calls and hurried back to see the new fireman. He was a nice-looking boy in a new straw hat and a fine new suit, standing helplessly where someone had left him near the Butterfly. I showed him where to get into his overalls. Old Phil was in the roundhouse ready to go, but he wouldn't speak to the boy and made faces to me behind the new fireman's back, pointing his thumbs in derision at the matting sleeve-guards that protected the boy's white cuffs. He beckoned me out of earshot.

"Nobby," he asked, "what do you think of him? Ain't a jury in the world would convict you if you hit him with a slash bar."

Contrarily I began to feel sorry for the boy, so I showed him how to wipe the jacket of the boiler and fill the fire-box, putting a tier of wood across the front. He looked dubiously at Fly, settled on a bed of waste in front of the driver's seat, but I assured him that Fly would scorn to take a bite of a tallow pot. Old Phil climbed in and grinned at me from the cab window, and I knew it wasn't going to be a good run for that boy with the soft girl's hands.

Next day I stayed around and waited until the boy signed in. He was a pitiful sight, with his face parboiled, his longish blond hair (that had been parted so neatly in the middle) singed, and his fingers wrapped in bandages so thick that he couldn't close his hands.

"Do you like the job?" I asked.

Instead of kicking my teeth in, he replied politely that he thought it was awful, especially the horrible, cross old man; but that he was going to stick it out until Saturday, because Mr. Maynard had been so earnest about his making railroading his career. When I asked if he thought that there was any chance of my getting the job, he promised to speak to Mr. Maynard about it; and since I had been kind, he would do it right away, before they put on someone else.

Next day the Superintendent sent for me. He, too, was doubtful about my age and weight, but I looked at him with the most wistful expression that I could manage and told him how hard I was trying to make a home for my mother. If he would only give me the chance, we could set up housekeeping in our own place. (This was the story I had already told John Bailey, and it was substantially true, except that we had rented part of a house the minute I got the calling job. Mother went out nursing whenever she had a chance, but no matter how little there might be in her shabby black purse, there was always food in the kitchen.)

Mr. Maynard was impressed, but he held out for a promise that I would go to night school and get an education. That was easy. I would have agreed to read the Bible backwards every night and say the multiplication table standing on my head.

On Monday morning Phil was grinning clear across his face.

"Move over, Fly," he ordered. "Make way for a fireman that *is* a fireman. Do you think you can keep the steam up in this calliope? The old girl will run like a scared cat with a couple of cars, but she balks with a load." I nodded and climbed up proudly beside him in the cab, laying two or three sticks ready on the deck.

George came over and grinned at me enviously, Old Phil gave her a little steam and the Butterfly bucked into the yard and eased into seven flatcars crowded with St. Regis Indians. The brakeman coupled us on, stuck the flag markers on the back of the caboose, and we were a train. The conductor, an old-timer like Phil, who had been pulled from the "extra" list, came over from the yard office. He said we were all clear, and we waited for the green light on the switch. A moment later we got the "go ahead." Phil let her out gently, I could hear the ripple of grunts that ran from car to car as he took up the slack, and we were out on the main line.

We stayed on the main stem until we got out of town. Then Phil shut off the steam and coasted, while the shack who had been riding the engine with us jumped down, ran ahead, unlocked a switch that threw us onto a spur and waited beside the track until we ran in and cleared the main. Then he "lined up" the switch, sprinted after the caboose and swung up by her grab iron. Phil gave her steam, and the Butterfly leapt, buckety-buck, toward the gravel pit.

I had built up such a hot fire that we didn't need more than a couple of logs and a poke with the slash bar before we reached the cut. When we had run into a newly laid switch and backed the flatcars into the pit, Phil told me to take a look at the fire while he checked the pressure. The Butterfly was so old that she didn't have a steam gauge.

The Indians—about a hundred and fifty of them—piled off the flatcars, and I stared with curiosity, for the only red man I had seen was a wooden one in front of a cigar store. Mr. Maynard had brought these down from Ogdensburg the week before, and they were living in old boxcars and coaches at the edge of the yard, but I hadn't caught a glimpse of them. Silently, with no undue haste, they dropped from the flats and picked up their shovels— tall loose-jointed men with closed faces, and not a smile among them. The section boss, a shouting Irishman, ran about barking orders, but they paid no more attention to him than if he were a buzz-fly.

"You should have seen these wooden babies lay rails; they're the lightning kids. But they're a washout with a shovel. Every time one of 'em opens his mouth, the whole tribe stops work to listen."

Calling to Fly, Old Phil climbed down to stretch his legs, leaving me to watch the fire. After fussing with the Butterfly's grease cups and looking under her drivers, he stuck the oilcan back into the cab.

"When they want me, just give me a whistle," he said. Pretty soon I saw him heading for the caboose and a game of poker with old Kidney-foot, the conductor.

We made four trips a day to the swamp, which we were filling in to be part of the yard, and the firing wasn't hard; but even with Phil's tips about pitching the timber, the three-foot lengths of hardwood cut my fingers so deeply that the welts still show as diagonal white ridges on their inner sides. The trick was to open the fire door, throw in two or three sticks and slam the door shut in a hurry before the draft scalped you. In these old balloon stacks it was so strong that it nearly pulled off your ears. If Phil told the Sunday School kid to keep the door open, no wonder he singed his hair and tore his fingers to the bone.

By the end of the week I knew every whim of the Butterfly: her reluctance to answer to the throttle, her bucking when she picked up speed and her distressing habit of leaking steam at every joint; but I loved her and kept her as shining as if she were pulling a fast freight from Buffalo.

For several weeks we ran without incident, and every once in a while Phil would let me handle the engine, pulling the Butterfly a few feet or backing her up to "spot" a new car for a load. He was continually tinkering with her, afraid that she would fall apart and he would lose his run. Sometimes he scorched the rails and made the Indians shimmy on the flats, cutting pretty fine our five minutes' clearance ahead of a scheduled train; and I could see a gleam in his eyes as we bumped and clattered into the yards. But this did not happen often, for he was careful of the rickety old dame.

On the last day of the month, their payday, some of the Indians loosened up and grunted a word or two. At four o'clock on the minute Irish Mike called them off, and they began to load their shovels in the cars. On the way home the Butterfly bucked and rattled a little more than usual, and Phil kept holding his ear down and asking if I heard something knocking, but I didn't hear a thing. As we slowed down to take the main line, Phil and Kidney-foot looked up and down the track for a plume of smoke, knowing that they had twenty minutes on Black River Jack's afternoon passenger.

"Plenty of time," said Kidney-foot. "Nothing coming, and Jack won't see our tail."

As the brakeman threw the switch, Phil opened up; but just as the Butterfly stuck her nose over on the main track, she let out a croak and a roar that bounced me back into the tender. Phil yelled at me through a white cloud of steam, but I couldn't hear what he said. Picking myself up from the woodpile, I saw that he had set the brakes and shut off the steam before he climbed over the side. The conductor was already beside the drivers.

"Knock off a cylinder head?" he asked.

Phil nodded, his nose close to the wheel. "Whole head blown off. We'll have to take her down."

Kidney-foot called the shack who was ambling up from the caboose.

"Go up the track and flag—and if you short flag, Old Phil will break your back. You know what a grouch he is." Kidney-foot went to the cab and grabbed the red flag from its nails over my seat and hobbled in the other direction.

"Sorry I can't help you, Phil," he called back, "but I'd better cover the front end."

Phil set to work, while I handed the tools. The Indians got down and stood about, sullen-eyed; and Big Mike herded them away from the engine when he was not helping Phil with his weight on a wrench.

Fifteen minutes, seventeen—the main rod was disconnected and the crosshead blocked; but the bolts were rusty, and the two men grunted as they took turns with the wrench. While they were disconnecting the valve stem, we heard Number 17 thundering down the track. Her whistle shrieking and her brakeshoes squawking as they grabbed the wheels, she pulled to an angry stop; but neither Phil nor Mike looked up. The valve was blocked. Old Phil climbed into the cab, threw the reverse lever and the Butterfly limped back a few feet onto the spur. The second she cleared it, I threw the switch, and the passenger snorted by, her cylinder cocks spitting as she gathered speed. Black River Jack leaned out of the cab and stuck four fingers at us.

"Only four minutes late," muttered Phil. "Serve him right if I kept him here all night."

"What do you want to do?" asked Kidney-foot, rolling up the flag.

"I can get her in," Phil answered, "if we crawl."

Mike rounded up the Indians, Kidney-foot gave the highball and we started off, creeping gingerly along the track. The crippled old Butterfly dragged like a paralytic, with one side down; but somehow Phil pushed her along. The cab was like a graveyard. I built up the fire and walked across to put a hand on Phil's arm.

"It wasn't anything you could help."

He didn't answer but pulled out his red bandanna and blew a great snort through his nose.

In the yard John Bailey was waiting for us, his face red with vexation above his crimped beard. "So you blew a cylinder."

"Yeh, I blew a cylinder, and you know damned well there isn't another runner on the board coulda kept that ash-can from falling apart as long as this." Old Phil turned his back and stalked away, holding himself as straight as a slash bar, with Fly loping at his heels.

3. Death on the Butterfly

THE GRAVEL TRAIN WAS LAID OFF FOR A week, but not entirely on account of the Butterfly. That Saturday night when the Indians were paid, they took on all the firewater in Utica and made such whoopee that the mayor called out the entire police force and the volunteer firemen. While their money lasted, the redskins howled through the streets; and when their jeans were empty, they staggered back to the yard to sleep it off. On Monday morning not more than a half dozen of them showed up—not enough to send out a train, even if John Bailey could have found an engine.

So while Mr. Maynard shipped the sick Indians back to Ogdensburg and waited for a gang of Italians from New York, Old Phil and Fly and I went fishing. The Mohawk was a low, muddy stream and dirty; even the scrub oaks along the bank were coated with dust. But we found a sycamore on a little bluff, baited our hooks from the can of fishing worms that we had dug in Phil's back yard, and stuck our poles into the ground while we lay down to wait—Phil in the sun, I in the shade, with the visors of our caps pulled over our eyes.

Fly dug a hole, rolled in the dust to make himself comfortable and went to sleep, while Phil and I stretched lazily, looking up at the tiny insects and specks of dust floating between us and the china-blue sky. Neither of us said very much.

After a while Phil began to talk about the old railroading days, before there were headlights or water tanks. When they wanted to run at night—the idea itself was daring—they hitched a flatcar to the front of an engine, covered it with sand, built a fire of pine knots on it for a headlight, and ran plunging into the dark like a smoking, red-eyed dragon. The engineer could see very little of the track through the smoke and flames, but there was not much danger of meeting anything except a frightened cow. For water they stopped at any handy creek and lugged it to the engine in canvas bags.

Phil had been a brakeman before the Civil War, when he was a young man and thumbed his nose at danger; but in those days a shack didn't have a chance. Pin couplings killed more men than Rebel bullets. As he remembered it, the war was a railroad picnic. He tore up rails in Georgia and South Carolina, prying them loose with long, home-made iron claws, and built fires on the rails until they were hot enough to wrap around a tree. After the fighting was over, he came back to railroading, but stuck to firing until he was set up with an engine. He had tried everything— even steamboating—but he "didn't fancy being burned up on a river." Give him a long, clear stretch and another runner eating up the smoke on a passing-track, racing for the pike, yelling insults out the window, their hands pulling out the throttles. Even now, with an engine that didn't have the pip and with green boards ahead, he could scorch the cinders with the best of them. If old John Bailey wasn't such a grandmammy about his engines—he and his curlpaper beard!

Every day of that week we went fishing and talked about engines, and on Sunday night John Bailey called us to take out the Butterfly. She had been turned out of the shop with her main rod coupled up and a new cylinder head. Phil and Kidney-foot smiled at each other as the conductor brought over the order, and we pulled out the flatcars. The Italians were a happy lot. They made so much noise that you would think they were all practicing to be barkers at a fair. At the cut they never stopped jabbering. Sometimes they sang, but they were also good with the shovels. Only one of them, the interpreter, spoke English, and he trailed Big Mike, trying to understand his cuss words.

On their first payday the Italians spent a nickel or two for a glass of beer, but they were no boozers. With their money they bought hats—all of the same kind, little round sailors such as small boys wear to Sunday School, with black ribbon streamers hanging down the back. They were a queer sight in their purplish-brown corduroy jackets (damp with sweat on these hot spring days, for they never took them off); loaves of bread with pieces of meat tied to them sticking out of their hip pockets; and their broad, bearded faces, some of them as fierce as a pirate's, grinning happily under these foolish hats. Some of them had gold hoops dangling from their ears.

When Phil saw the hats, he doubled over the reverse

lever, and I thought he was going to choke. "What are we hauling?" he sputtered. "A load of blackballers on a Sunday School picnic? I declare, Nobby, I'm all mixed up."

Through June they clawed into the gravel pit, while Old Phil took it easy. He climbed up the bank with Fly and went to sleep, leaving me to mind the engine. I sat proudly on the runner's seat and moved the Butterfly up a few feet whenever the caboose signalled her ahead. All day I hung out of the right-hand window, pretending to watch the shack give me a back-up signal or a low swing of the arm, a "washout" telling me to stop; and I imagined that I was taking the Butterfly for a real run, curling the rails on a clear stretch, easing her to a stop with her express car spotted smack in front of the agent's door (she was always pulling a fast train with an express car). Oh, I could run the Butterfly if I had the chance, could make her pick up slack as smoothly as a girl waltzing with a glass of water on her head.

Sometimes I shared my pie with the two little water boys and tried to teach them English. When I let them ride in the cab, I put their hands on the throttle and taught them to repeat the word "throttle" after me, then "lever" and "igniter," trying to make them engineers. The littlest one, who squealed when he stepped on the water hose, thinking it a snake, is now the president of a bank in Utica.

When we reached the gravel pit one fine June morning, the Italians did not go to work. They climbed onto the gravel and stretched out with their little hats over their faces, or sat on the edge of the flats, dangling their stocky legs. One started to sing *O Sole Mio*, and in a minute all their voices bounced back from the walls of the pit. Irish Mike raged and shouted, but they laughed in his face. Kidney-foot asked the interpreter what was up, and he learned that it was a strike.

"The boys ain't satisfied with a dollar a day," said the interpreter. "They want a dollar and a quarter, like they pay on the West Shore road."

Phil said I might as well let the fire die, as it looked like trouble. He and Kidney-foot climbed the bank and walked into the woods, taking Fly with them; but the brakie and I stood on the edge of the pit and watched.

One of the Italians, a bushy fellow with gold loops in his ears, found a broom in the caboose and began to sweep the floors of the cars. Before he had finished, a couple of handcars came rolling up from town, filled with more Italians waving the same little hats, the ribbons sticking out in the breeze. On the front car we could see a barrel of beer and a monkey sitting on a hand organ.

When they reached the train, the organ-grinder jumped off and climbed on the nearest flatcar, with the monkey holding onto his ear. As he started to grind, the men in the pit scrambled onto the cars and danced, their boots thumping accompaniment to the tunes. They waved to us, inviting us to come down; so the shack and I rolled over the bank and joined the dance. The hand organ tinkled, a dusty fellow with his shirt open to the waist held out his hands, we stamped around and around, intoxicated by the whirling, our knees limbered by the heat and our faces gleaming with sweat. Handle-bar mustaches whipped into my eyes, elbows dug into my side. When I was drunk with whirling, I backed toward the organ-grinder, trying to get my breath.

"Hey, wanta play?" he asked. My partner slapped me happily on the back and danced away, while the organ-grinder threw the strap of the box over my head and took his monkey to make the rounds of the cars. Limply I cranked, while the blood danced in my ears to the tune of the monkey box.

After a while the frolic slowed down, the men opened the keg of beer and sat on the edge of the cars gnawing their loaves of bread, their mustaches covered with foam. Pete, the shack, and I got out our lunch boxes and climbed into the caboose, where we ate our pie and stretched out, drowsy and content. But just as we had found a soft spot on the floor for a trick of sleep, we heard a great commotion on the flats and the scraping of boots on gravel. I looked out and saw two new handcars coming up the track. They were near enough for us to distinguish the blue uniforms of the police. The last of the Italians was scrambling up the bank and disappearing in the woods.

Shaking ourselves, we climbed out to see Big Mike and a half-dozen cops unload. Mike must have walked back to town to get the Law; none of us had thought of him or missed him. He ordered me to get into the cab and toot for Phil; but the steam was down, and I had to build up the fire again. Mike cupped his hands, let out a mighty yell, and Phil and Kidney-foot came out of the woods. They all stood around and talked, but there was nothing to be done, for the Italians had taken to the woods like so many rabbits. By the time the handcars were loaded on the flats, the Butterfly was steaming and ready to take the officers back to town. Old Phil and Kidney-foot consulted their timecards and saw that they had ten minutes headway on Hiki's fast train with the coaches for New York. Phil climbed into the cab and I stuck out my head for the highball.

"Feelin' smart, Nobby? Can you hit the fire door with the timber if I show these cops how the old girl can kick her heels? We'll teach 'em to interfere with a peaceful, law-abiding strike!" He looked down to see that Fly was comfortable and anchored himself on his seat.

Old Phil was not a union man, I knew, and had little patience with united action, but the thought of coercion raised his temperature. On general principles he was against the cops.

He didn't open up on the spur, giving me a chance to get up steam; but when there was no show of smoke at the switch, and we got onto the main stem, he asked for all the old Butterfly had. She shimmied, and I reeled when I tried to throw in the wood. I wondered about the officers in the caboose, which Old Phil was slinging about like a can on the end of a mad dog's tail. We took the curves on half our wheels, but I chucked on some sand and we held to the rails. Kidney-foot signalled us to slow down, but Phil paid no heed, and the telegraph poles shot by like a picket fence.

"Put on your tender brake!" he shouted outside the yard, and when I had climbed back down, he was mincing the Butterfly up to the yard office as sedate as an old lady going to church. The cops rolled out and straightened their clothes.

"For half a bit," the sergeant threatened, "I'd run you into the cooler."

Old Phil glanced around to see that John Bailey wasn't at his window and patted the sergeant on the arm.

"Nonsense, pal, it was good for your liver. Come over to John Collins' and we'll have a drink."

By July the swamp was filled, and the Butterfly was ordered out to take the Italians ditching. This was more like a real run, for Alder Creek was about thirty miles from Utica, and at Remson we had to pull up a hill that took a lot of steam. Phil showed me the order before he stuck it into his jeans: "Wildcat between Utica and Boonville," it said. In those days train orders were brief and casual. If old Phil were to take out the Butterfly on that run today, his order would read:

Extra North, Eng. one will meet Extra South, Eng. two at Alder Creek.
    Correct
  Sign Conductor
    Engineer

But the old orders fired a boy's imagination. There was something thrilling in the thought of taking out a wildcat.

At Alder Creek we stayed on the main track until it was time to make way for a regular; then we took the siding while she streaked by. But if we expected a meet with another wildcat when on the job, we sent out a flagman and didn't call off the "gandy dancers" (that's what we called the section hands) until she actually showed her smoke.

All day long the Italians cleaned out the cuts that winter rains had filled. Phil gossiped with Kidney-foot in the caboose, or took Fly and walked into a white birch grove for a nap. I kept the steam up and handled the Butterfly. Once I even ran her into Boonville to file a message for John Bailey.

It was farming country, hills and pasture, with now and then a grove of trees or a corn patch. Phil knew the farmer who lived in the yellow house that we could see across a field, and sometimes he went over for a glass of cider. One hot morning he said that the Lord was calling him to go fishing, so he whistled to Fly and took a roll of line from under his seat.

"If you have to move, Nobby," he warned me, "ring the bell before·you start. Now don't forget. Be careful, won't you? If you want me, blow the whistle. I'll tell Kidney-foot where I've gone."

I tossed in the wood and worked the Butterfly all day, answering the brakeman's signals, running her in and out of the siding. At noon Kidney-foot and the shacks and I ate our lunch under a clump of birches. It was so hot that our jeans were as wet as our skin.

"You're a good boy, Nobby," Kidney-foot told me, languidly chewing the end of a feathered grass that he used to brush the gnats away. "You're a pretty good runner already, the way you make this old rattletrap step around." This was sweet praise, for Kidney-foot had been everything—shack, tallow pot, runner of fast freights, even conductor of a passenger train riding the cushions.

We got back to work. The sun rolled over to the other side of the track, and the Butterfly was so hot that it scorched your hand to touch her metal. By three o'clock Phil had not come back, and Kidney-foot came along looking worried.

"It's almost time to start to town," he said. "Think you'd better give the old goat a toot?"

As I lifted my hand to the cord, we looked across the pasture and there came Phil with the farmer on one side and a hired man on the other. Even with their help he was finding it hard to navigate. Kidney-foot wanted to take the throttle and let Phil sleep on the fireman's side of the cab; but Phil would have none of it, muttering that he would be all right if they would hoist him onto his seat.

"You get back to your own end," he ordered Kidney-foot, with a tongue so thick that the words would hardly form. "Nobby will look after me. You see there's water in her, Nobby, won't you? You take care of Old Phil. By God, sonny, I don't know what I'd do without you."

Reluctantly Kidney-foot went back to the caboose and signalled for the crew to get aboard. I hung out and watched for the highball. Phil gave her a shot of steam, and the Butterfly lurched forward. We were on the siding where I had wooded up and taken water, and I wondered if he would slow down for the switch. He did, and coasted easily while the shack climbed off and on.

When we were on the iron, I kept an anxious eye on Phil. His head nodded and he slumped on the box, but his hand was steady on the throttle, as if it had an intelligence of its own. I measured the steam. It was high and the fire red-hot, so we clanked through Remson without having to put in wood. Phil didn't look out, but I caught the signals and knew we had a clear track. Later I opened the fire door, tossed in a couple of logs and gave the ashes a hasty spreading, afraid that the blast of heat would be bad for Phil.

As I pulled out the slash bar, I heard a thud and felt Phil bump against me. His head had hit the top of the open furnace door; a great raw wound was gouged across his cheek. Slamming the door to, I pushed Phil back with my foot and grabbed for the throttle. We were getting into Trenton Falls. The telegrapher at the station came out on the platform as I coasted up, and I yelled for him to throw us into a siding. With the blood pounding in my temples so hard that I could scarcely see, I eased the Butterfly past the switch, looked back to see that the caboose had cleared and set the brake. Reaching for the bell cord, I yanked a series of whistles that sounded like a call for a riot squad. Then I got down on my knees and straightened out Old Phil.

Kidney-foot came running and stuck in his head, followed by the brakeman and the operator.

"What's the matter? What's happened to Phil?" I looked up, too frightened to speak. Kidney-foot climbed over me, felt Phil's hand and yelled to the operator to get a doctor. We carried Phil to the caboose and laid him on the bunk, followed by Fly, who whined anxiously at my heels. Old Phil wasn't breathing, but I wouldn't believe that he was dead. The gandy dancers, like anxious children, stood in a bunch behind the caboose, shaking their earrings and drawing on cold pipes.

In a few minutes we saw the doctor jump out of his buggy behind the station and run across the field, bumping his bag against his knees. He knelt over Phil and felt his heart, then stood up and wiped the moisture from his spectacles. A stroke, he said. Phil was probably dead before he struck the furnace door. Kidney-foot thanked the doctor and pulled a dollar from a thin, oily wad.

"We'd better be getting on," he said, with a gesture to

Mike to load his crew. "It'll be hard to tell the old lady. Want to drive her, Nobby?" he asked me. "It's downhill the rest of the way, and all you have to do is coast. Pete can fire for you. I'll stay back in the doghouse with Old Phil."

I went forward and climbed into the cab, my teeth chattering so hard that I bit my tongue to keep them still. Waiting for Black River Jack to bring through Number 14, I sat in the driver's seat with my numb fingers on the throttle. The passenger whistled for the station and threw off a bag of mail. Jack looked across at me and waved.

"Hello, Eagle-eye," he called.

Before his tail was out of sight, Kidney-foot signalled me to back out on the iron. Fingers on the throttle, eyes glued to the road, ears cocked for strange and dangerous noises in the general rumble and clatter, I tried to remember all that Phil had taught me; but the rest of the drive was a blur, and I didn't come to until the flats were cut off in the yard and the Butterfly was on the turntable.

John Bailey was waiting when I stumbled out of the cab. He patted my arm.

"You're all right, Nobby, you brought her in like an old-timer. Now you go ahead and tell Phil's old lady. Kidney-foot and I will get a carriage and bring Old Phil as soon as we can; and we'll look after Fly, he won't leave the caboose. But you tell her first. And tell her, Nobby, that the boys will take care of everything."

I nodded and went across the yard, dragging my feet as if I were half asleep. Clumps of wild asters were blooming along the dump, and the house stood off by itself as clear and sharp as if it had been cut out and stuck on a blue and yellow sunset.

When I opened the gate, the robin flew down from her box and swung on the ribbon, tinkling the bell. The old lady came to the door.

"Why, it's Nobby," she said. "Where's Phil?"

My tongue stuck to my mouth and my lips were so dry that I couldn't speak. She looked at my face and drew back, her eyes so large that they seemed to swallow her thin, pinched cheeks.

"Is he dead?" she asked.

I nodded.

"And they sent you to tell me. Poor Nobby." She went into the kitchen and brought me a doughnut. I took it and ran across the dump, sobbing and running as if my heart would burst.

4. On the Main Iron

ON THE DAY OF OLD PHIL'S FUNERAL, THE shops and yard were as deserted as if it were the Fourth of July. Everybody who was not actually out on a train came to his wife's house. They walked gingerly across the dump in their "chicken skin" Sunday shoes and jammed the front room so full that they stood packed against the walls. Baldy and Rubberguts and old John Bailey wore tall silk hats, with their B. L. E. (Brotherhood of Locomotive Engineers) emblems dangling from the watch chains that stretched like cables across their somber black vests. Pete, the robin, swung on the bell and chattered impatiently while the parson read the service; and Fly howled in the back yard, where he was tied to a chicken house.

The old lady gave me an anxious glance, and I went out to comfort Fly. He sniffed at my fingers, and I was glad to stay with him until they carried the coffin out through the broken front gate—John Bailey in the lead, with Kidney-foot in a frock coat so long that it almost caught his heels. Then I followed the procession a long way off, but turned away when it came to Water Street; for my throat hurt and my eyes smarted. Mother gave me some hot chicken broth, made from the bones of the old hen that we had eaten for dinner, and told me to cry if I wanted to.

"Don't be afraid of being a sissy," she said. "It will do you good. No matter what faults the old man had, he was your friend."

For a long time I thought about Phil at odd moments when I passed the Butterfly gathering dust in a corner of the roundhouse, her brass already so dull that it looked like tarnished silver; or when I saw Kidney-foot pulling out on a roustabout. The ditching was finished, the Italians had returned to New York and I was working in the shop until I could persuade John Bailey to send me out firing again. In slow seasons all the men who weren't on regular runs could work in the shop, but they didn't like it because of the poorer pay. A railroader in those days was so handy with the wrench and cold chisel that he could do almost everything short of making a new engine, and he wouldn't have been entirely hopeless at that.

The shop was a great, wide shack with the sun pouring in through the open door and windows all around. Clouds of dust and metal filings danced in the light, and the place was full of the sound of hammering and the grunts and shouts of men wrestling with heavy engine parts. The floor was cluttered with headlights, brass trimmings of engines, flat wheels, and dismembered boilers. It made you feel arrogant and at the same time sad to walk safely among these crippled hulks, which were usually so full of snorting power.

On one side were yellow passenger cars trimmed inside with carved curlicues, very elegant, and upholstered with bright blue plush. They were heated with potbellied wood stoves with silver rails and isinglass doors, which were shined until they looked like black diamonds. The boxcars were gaudy but not so interesting as those that I had seen on the New York Central line when I was a child. On their pale-gray sides were painted portraits in huge ovals, one to a car. I remember best the likeness of the Governor of Massachusetts against a Turkey-red background—an overpowering fellow, looking out full face with a high white collar and black whiskers chopped off by the edge of the frame. The Governor of Maine was more of a dandy, a regular profile against robin's-egg blue —his whiskers, like those of John Bailey, looking as if they had been waved with a curling iron.

But our own Black River cars were by no means subdued when they came out of the paint shop in new blue-and-yellow coats. I would have enjoyed slathering them with paint, but that was a specialized job, so I was put to unscrewing the bolts of crippled engines that had to be taken down. I liked the smell of turpentine and grease and the screeching of files on steel, and I would have been happy in the shop if I hadn't been so eager to get back on the high iron. Every morning I stopped by the board to see if John Bailey could have marked me up and the new call boy forgotten to let me know.

George Hughes also was keeping an eye on the board, for John had promised to send him out firing as soon as business picked up in the fall. Meanwhile we sweated under our coatings of ashes and grease, and on our days off went swimming in the Mohawk with a gang of young shacks and tallow pots. It was a muddy swimming hole, so shallow that when we dived we were likely to bump our heads on a rock; but in August the water was cool, and whatever breeze there was rippled soothingly over our bare, dripping skin. After we had splashed for a while, we loafed in the shade and drank beer from a small keg that we had carried down with us—it cost a dollar and a half but we raised the money by all chipping in.

On one such sultry day George was telling us how his cousin, a shack on the Boston & Maine, rode the tops of a heavy freight in an ice storm. Pulling up a mountain, three rear cars broke loose and slithered down the track. Singlehanded the brakeman rode the runaway cars and set the brakes so tight that later it took three men to loose the binders. The cars slowed up in the valley, with every wheel flat, but on the rails; and the cousin was so nearly frozen by the draft of icy wind they made coming down the mountain that one ear broke off in his hand. We let George talk, too lazy to match him with a better one.

As we lay on the dusty grass, occasionally fanning the gnats with plumed grass, a strange head was thrust out of a thicket down the bank, a handful of tousled carrot-red hair sticking out from a dirty face. The leaves parted and a man crawled out. He was a hobo by the looks of him. Everything about him was the color of dirty brass, except two intensely blue, inquisitive eyes.

"Hello, pals," he called, giving us a salute. "Did I smell beer? Here's your chance to get the biggest bargain of your life. You see before you the great Billsborough, the extraordinary artist with the needle, direct from New

York City. I'll make you a bargain, gents: for twenty-five cents, just one quarter, and a mug of beer, I'll tattoo you with any two of these handsome designs." He shrugged out of his coat and stood naked to the waist. Turning slowly, he exhibited on his arms and back and chest the most complete picture gallery that we had ever seen.

"You first, mate." He fastened his intense blue eyes on me, for I was already feeling in my coat for a quarter, my spending money for the week. "What'll it be? Any two. How about a gal in tights and a heart and arrow with your sweetheart's name?"

But I was more conservative and settled on an American Eagle for one arm and *E Pluribus Unum* for the other. I would have liked the handsome design of crossed snakes, which he had on the small of his back, or a sailing ship; but he would do no more for a quarter.

First "the great Billsborough" drank his beer—the dregs of the keg, but he gulped it down and wiped his mouth with the back of a dirty hand. Then he sat down on the bank and pulled out of his coat a stubby piece of India ink (which looked like black chalk) and a half of a walnut shell. Dusting out the shell with his thumb, he rubbed a bit of the chalk into it, spit tobacco juice on the ink and worked the mixture with the end of his little finger. Then with three needles tied together he drew the designs on my arms and pricked them in.

"Who next, mates?" He tipped up the keg of beer and, seeing that it was empty, wasted no time in persuasion. The boys had hung over him with curiosity while he decorated me, but they did not come forward with their quarters; so the great Billsborough threw his coat over his arm and swaggered down the bank, giving the sailing ships and naked women a lifelike motion.

My arms were sore for a day or two, but I went about with my sleeves rolled up, hoping that Baldy would notice the designs. Whenever I could manage it, I hung about the roundhouse to see the crews taking out the engines or coasting them in from a run and spotting them on the turntable. There was plenty of work to be done here too, so John Bailey didn't care.

As I was cleaning the flues of a boiler one morning and entertaining George by drawing a whiskered portrait of John on the sooty fire side of the smokebox door, Baldy came in—spotless as ever, in the daily clean white shirt and fresh laundered overalls (he never hid his snowiness under the denim jackets that are the working uniform of train-men). With him was John Bailey. He and John walked over to me and, before I could slam the door, stood look-ing at the handsome whiskers. George snickered and backed away to his own job, but neither John nor Baldy cracked a smile.

"How about putting in my grate for me, Nobby?" Baldy asked. His engine was a little beauty, the newest on the road; but the door to the firebox was so small that a big man couldn't crawl in to set the grate. Usually his fireman did it, a lean fellow who could have squeezed through a knothole; but Baldy told me that he had fallen off the tank and hurt his back.

While I was in the belly of this handsome new smoke-eater, a dazzling idea leaped into my mind. It was fantastic,

I knew; but Baldy liked me, and it was just possible that he might let me fire for him! Wriggling backward out of the door, I heard the two men talking.

"I don't know what you are going to do," said John. "All the firemen off duty are at Trenton Falls on a picnic. We might try to get old Piccadilly."

As I straightened up, I stepped behind John Bailey and looked at Baldy with such a fierce longing that the ends of his mustache curled with amusement.

"Hell, no," he answered. "Old Piccadilly's likely to shake to pieces going up Remson Hill. How about Nobby here? I could take him out for to-night. What you say, Nobby? Do you think you could keep her hot?"

I nodded, too excited to speak. John Bailey shook his head dubiously.

"You know he's too young, Ed; but it's your responsibility. If you get stuck on the hill, don't wire me for a helper. Your passengers can walk to Watertown." He told me to go home, get something to eat and be back at four o'clock.

I ran all the way and burst into the kitchen to tell mother that I must dress up, I was going out on the passenger. While I gulped my dinner, she laid out my best blue-and-white checked shirt and black bow tie. With my hair plastered with water and shoes shined, I hurried back to the roundhouse.

Number 22 was already on the turntable; spitting steam. In a few minutes Baldy came in. He and the conductor compared watches, picked up the orders and we all climbed aboard the engine, the two brakemen riding on the steps. Baldy gave her a whisper of steam, and we slid into the yard to take on wood and water. At the wood-pile the whole crew worked, piling up logs in the tender. Baldy stacked them in the gangway and I filled the firebox. Gently we backed into the train: four bright yellow coaches trimmed with black, a mail car, and, on the tail, a "combo" (an express and baggage car). The head shack dropped in the coupling pin, and we strutted into the station.

Across Baldy's shoulders I could see the passengers waiting on the platform—fashionable ladies in bonnets set above frizzed bangs, their trailing skirts hiked up over bustles, their parasols fluttering; and men with broad hats and waxed mustaches—summer people going to the Thousand Islands. But I was as grand as they; for I was not yet seventeen, and I was firing the fastest scorcher on the line.

After we got the highball and Baldy eased us out, picking up the slack without a bump, he nodded to the steam gauge. "Now, Nobby, you keep your eyes on the steam and see that we carry a hundred and forty pounds. When she gets high and ready to pop, you can open the door a little; but the minute she begins to drop, go to work. You'll have to fire like hell to pull us up to Remson."

Didn't I know it! On that hill I had slit my fingers almost to the bone. Marcy, Stittsville, Holland Patent—we made short, impatient stops, and I took advantage of every one to stoke the fire.

We had no air brakes but we coasted to a fine stop. The baggageman and the trainmen manned the hand brakes and were so well trained that they turned the wheels on the instant that Baldy whistled for brakes. It was my job to tend the tank brake; so as we slid into a station, I grabbed the club (a tough piece of hickory shaped liked a baseball bat), stuck it through the wheel and at the signal from Baldy gave it a wrench that clamped the shoes tight on the resisting wheels. At Marcy I set the wheel so hard that Baldy had to climb down from his seat and throw his whole weight on one end of the club before we could get it loose.

Baldy didn't say anything or pay much attention to me, except to call orders, until we got up the hill at Remson. Number 17 didn't stop at Trenton Falls, except to leave passengers; and on this run we whistled through without cutting off steam. As we hooted in the outskirts of Remson (a large town with rows of little back yards and gardens flanking the tracks), Baldy shouted to me, "Open the firebox door." I threw it open and watched anxiously while the steam went down.

"It's all right, boy," he explained while we stood in the station. "Got to leave the door open to lower the steam pressure when we come into a big station. When she spits and pops, she's likely to scare the horses; and we can't take a chance of doing that. It's important. Don't you ever forget."

I had not seen Remson at train time, so I leaned out of the window and watched the people walking up and down the platform. There was a great bustle of climbing off and on the coaches, cabbies shouting and people milling about the hacks and private carriages standing at the hitching-rail. Opposite me a girl with long curls under a flower-covered bonnet was standing beside a pony cart. I waved, and she smiled shyly back at me.

"Look, papa, look," I heard her say to the man beside her. "That's just a boy." The man glanced at me and smiled too. When we pulled out, I shouted good-by and waved again. Baldy laughed.

"Some punkins, eh, Nobby?"

At Alder Creek, where we took wood and water, all the crew got off and helped wood up, even the deadheads riding the cushions. Just beyond the station was the siding into which I used to run the gravel train to get out of the way of the "regular."

When we are young, time is elastic and stretches on and on forever. It already seemed years since I had helped Old Phil into the cab of the Butterfly and listened to him mutter, "You'll take care of me, won't you, Nobby?" For weeks I kept wondering if there was anything else I could have done. But it was over now, life pushed along fast and I no longer saw the old man every time I went to sleep; but I thought of him as we wooded up, hoping he would be proud of me.

Boonville I remembered, with its abandoned locks and the decaying saloons and fancy houses, which had done a fine business when the timber boats came down from Carthage on their way to the Erie Canal; but after we left it, the way was new to me. We followed the twisting black line of the river around the hills to Carthage and then rode gently down through the high timber toward the St. Lawrence. Downgrade I did not have to fire so steadily, and Baldy too relaxed. When we had eased out of

Port Leyden and picked up our speed, he leaned back in the window and called in an imperious tone, "Boy, my teeth!" I was eyeing the steam gauge, and as I looked around, I nearly tripped over the slash bar. He was holding out to me a set of false teeth—the uppers held gingerly by the points of his fingers. They were dripping with tobacco juice.

"Wash them," he ordered, indicating with his head the tap on the water tank. I put them under the spigot and washed them off. Then he returned them to his mouth and smoothed his beard in the little mirror hung on the front wall of the engine. Four times between Utica and Watertown—every time he finished a chew of tobacco—he held them out to me with that lordly gesture.

"What a man," I thought. "What fastidiousness!" And I burned with admiration.

As I examined him sitting on the high seat, solid and handsome, his heavy white arm lying along the window, with the sleeve meticulously folded back to cut off the head of a tattooed lady, I could find only one imperfection in his magnificent person; a row of little pits around the base of his neck. It seemed almost as if he had been marked with smallpox there and nowhere else. What hair he had left, he wore long over these scars. All the engineers, I had noticed, wore their hair uncut on the back of the neck. Before I got to Watertown, I knew why. The pits were scars from the red-hot sparks that flew down into their collars.

As we shot through this new country, whistling for way stations, I caught a glimpse of rowdy little falls tumbling over saw-toothed rocks, and watched the forest swoop down to little white villages. When Baldy cut off the steam to drift down to Lowville, he said that it was time to oil the valves and cylinders. I knew what I was to do; climb out on the running board of the engine and open the cocks, so that the oil could be sucked from the cups into the steam chest. It looked simple enough when she was standing on the roundhouse track.

From the shelf on the boiler head I took the tallow pot, a handsome one with a spout like a teakettle and shiny brass bands around its black iron mouth. The tallow was warm enough to pour, so I grabbed the hand-hold and climbed onto the board, clinging there for a dizzy moment, trying not to fall off onto the ribbon of ballast shooting by on the roadbed, or against the hot jacket of the boiler. The grade was not steep, but the rails swooped down and around a hill, and the runners pounded in my ears and screeched as they took the curve. Holding myself there, with the wind cutting my face and blowing out my hair in a fan, I thought I was riding a runaway train; but I glanced back and saw Baldy in the cab, resting against the window and smiling at me. This was nothing, nothing at all. Shutting the cocks, I climbed back and nonchalantly threw in a couple of logs.

Playing tag with narrow Deer River, scuttering under the willows, we drove into Carthage, a city and a junction where we lost our coaches that went on to Ogdensburg and picked up new ones for Watertown. It was dusk. After we wooded up and took water, Baldy called to me for a piece of clean waste and polished the glass of his headlights before he lighted the whale-oil lamp. The beam fanned out along the roadbed in a yellow glow. While we tied onto the new cars, and the passengers from Watertown changed coaches, I walked back and stared at the people in the windows. They looked like shadow pictures against the pale squares of light made by the sperm tallow candles, which I could see flickering in their round glass globes.

"Come on, Nobby, stop gaping," Baldy called to me, looking at his watch. "We've got to step along." We were off around the Great Bend, but all I could see of it was the rails curving and running sidewise away from the cone of light. At Black River a shack held a couple of lanterns while we wooded up, and I opened the fire door to throw a light into the tender.

It was dark when we got to Watertown and put the engine in the roundhouse. Baldy patted me on the shoulder as he climbed out of the cab and went to wash up. A quarter of an hour later, he waved good-by and went uptown, a resplendent figure in his derby and black town clothes. He was a spender, the boys in the roundhouse said, and after a big dinner at the hotel, would sit around all evening in a discreet game of poker with the other lords of the road.

The conductor, the shacks, and the baggageman drifted away, with their shoes blacked and their hair plastered down. Everyone had some place to go except me. I washed up and came back to sit on the engine step, the pride oozing out of me. There was no one left in that dim, smelly barn except the roundhouse man. He was cross and lame, and when he came around to wipe off the engine after the fire had died, he seemed put out that I was just a boy. But when I helped him go over the rods and running gear, he felt sorry for me and asked if I would like to see the town.

We walked up a cobbled street lined with railroad stores and beer parlors. Stopping next a saloon, he opened a side door that gave onto a stairway, and we climbed to the second floor. His knock at one of the doors on the landing was answered by a fat girl with bad teeth and bleached hair, which showed dark around the roots. Another girl in a torn red calico dress got up from a sofa and gave the wiper a hug.

"Ah, ze brave Henri! Why you stay so long away?" The blonde said something to her in words that sputtered and ran together. I guessed they must be French. They looked me over, motioned me to the couch and paid no further attention to me.

The wiper threw a quarter on the table, and the girl in the red dress went downstairs for a pitcher of beer. The blonde rolled up the lid of an organ, which was draped with a piece of fly-specked yellow velvet, and began to sing words that I could not understand; but I guessed they were bawdy by the way she fluttered her eyelashes at the wiper. He went over and sat beside her on the stool, holding onto her while he pumped with his good foot. At every bar or two she giggled, slapped him and screamed, "Non, non!" when he pushed her too far off the bench.

The girl who had gone for the beer came back and set the stone pitcher in the middle of the table, the top of which was marked all over with rings. She brought out glasses and motioned to us. The wiper and the blonde untangled themselves from the organ stool and scuffled for the same chair. I got up from the couch where I had been rooted, with my cap still in my hand, and took a step toward the table; but I didn't like these sloppy girls with their frizzed hair, their jabbering to each other in a tongue I couldn't understand and their rough way of making a boy feel of no more account than a speck on their dirty glasses. Saying good night, I went out and closed the door. The wiper followed me onto the stairs.

"What's the matter, kid? You ain't bashful, are you?"

I shook my head. All I wanted was to get back to my engine.

There was a quarter in my pocket and, on the way to the roundhouse, I looked into the windows of the saloons, the only places where a man could get a sandwich; but I was disgusted with the thought of beer. Number 22 would be friendly and clean. So I laid Baldy's cushion on the deck and curled up on it—at least, as much of me as I could manage. But it was a long time before sleep came. My veins boiled with a heady exultation, and I saw myself firing an incredibly big engine, pulling up a mountain in the night, her runners pounding like thunder and her stack belching a plume of sparks as long as a comet's tail.

5. Rose of Cedarville Crossing

LTHOUGH JOHN BAILEY HELD FAIRLY strictly to seniority privileges, and all the firemen on the board had "whiskers" on me, I fired Number 22 for two weeks. When the older smoke-makers tried to buck me off the job, Baldy would have none of it. Every day when we had strained over the hump of Remson Hill and the wood was low, I practiced pitching it into the fire door from the back of the tender; but I wasn't good enough yet, and once Baldy swore when I hit his foot instead of the furnace mouth.

At oiling I was quick, and I managed to be out on the running board when we were drifting into a station, preening with the tallow pot before the curious eyes on the platform. The trick amused Baldy, and he humored my vanity so long as I was in the cab when he whistled for the brakes.

But at last his fireman's back was mended, and I was in the shop again, screwing and unscrewing nuts. John Bailey promised to do what he could for me, but George was still waiting for his chance, and the board was full of extras.

It was rumored on the stovepipe circuit that the Black

River Line was buying two new coal-burners, powerful engines for hauling heavy drags of freight. When they arrived, George and I looked them over on one of the roundhouse tracks: tremendous creatures with low runners and an extra pair of pony wheels. The running board seemed as high as a second story. Number 23 was my favorite, for no reason—they were exactly alike—and I nosed around her every time I could make an occasion to cross the roundhouse, looked at her large headlight, stuck my head into the furnace and examined her throttle and reverse lever. More than anything in the world I wanted to fire that engine, and I thought about it so constantly that I almost believed it might come true.

But John Bailey had other ideas.

"You've never fired a coal engine, son," he told me, "and they're twice as hard to manage as wood. They take more skill. I'm getting a couple of men from the Lackawanna to fire them—men who know coal."

That night when I ate my second piece of berry pie in savage gloom, mother asked what was the trouble. Had old John Bailey caught me out in some mischief and given me the sack? When I told her about Number 23, she said that if the Lackawanna men were coming to the Black River Line, why didn't I go to the Lackawanna?

Why not? There was only one reason: my awe of the Master Mechanic who controlled everything that rolled on the Utica branch. Tom Thatcher was a hard man with a quick temper and a cursing tongue. His teeth stuck out in front through a red, scraggly beard, and when he laughed, his breath hissed through the space between them.

One of his eyes was glass, and it followed you around with a malevolent stare; and yet they said at John Collins' that if you saw a kind expression on the Old Man's face, you were surely looking into his artificial eye. He was a good family man, and his wife had him under her thumb; but in the shop he had no thought for anything beyond his equipment. They said he'd rather have his engines kill a fireman any day than blow a cylinder.

Sunday morning I walked past the Lackawanna yard to reconnoiter. The Old Man's office was next to the roundhouse, and everybody in town knew that he never went to church; so I might be able to catch him alone in a softened mood. There he was, sitting at his desk behind the railing that the men called the "judgment bar." The door was open, and I went in, my hat in my hand, my head held high above the celluloid collar that was part of my Sunday outfit.

"Good morning, Mr. Thatcher."

The Old Man whirled around in his chair and glared at me—at least I thought he glared, but I was so hypnotized by the glass eye, a little larger and bluer than the other, that I couldn't be sure whether the mangy red whiskers hid a smile or a snarl.

"Good morning," he hissed through his teeth, like an engine blowing off steam. "And what do *you* want?"

When he heard that I wanted to go firing on the Lackawanna, he cocked his head a little and fixed the good eye on me in a contemptuous stare, making me conscious of my skimpy frame that was shooting up like a weed but tipped the scale at scarcely a hundred pounds.

"What makes you want to fire?" he demanded, with scorn for the colossal stupidity of such a notion.

Because I intended to be an engineer, I told him, and had already been firing on the Black River Line.

"Then why don't you stay there?" he flung at me, in a tone designed to end this futile conversation.

Because, I answered, the Lackawanna men were coming over from his road to run the new engines.

At this news the Old Man turned the full power of his headlight on me and sat forward in his seat. "And who," he asked, "may they be?"

"Humphrey O'Brien," I answered, "and . . ."

"Humphrey O'Brien," he interrupted. "Humphrey O'Brien!" Never have I heard such scorn in a human voice. "The drunken slob!" His tone disposed of Humphrey with an awful finality. "And who else?"

"Dan Kelly."

"Dan Kelly," he spit out the words. "Dirty Dan Kelly. Glad to be rid of him!"

Pleased with himself for having so neatly annihilated Humphrey and Dan, the Old Man parted his whiskers in what I took to be a smile.

"I'll think it over. Come back tomorrow morning." He turned around in the swivel chair and focussed his good eye on the order board, forgetting that I was there.

In the morning at seven o'clock I was back again. It was a busy place, engineers and firemen standing before the rail for orders, a meek clerk copying longhand in a huge ledger and the Old Man cussing the brainlessness of every eagle-eye who was taking out an engine. It made

John Bailey's corner in the Black River shop seem as peaceful as a graveyard. While the Old Man was kicking out his engineers, I had time to look around. The board was bigger and more impressive than John's and looked like a gigantic game board punched with rows of holes, in which sat wooden pegs with T-shaped heads. On each head was painted a name. When Thatcher made up his call list, he shifted the pegs back and forth from the "extra" list to the regular board as he needed them.

"So you're the boy who wants to learn how to fire," he shot at me, revolving his head sidewise to get me in range. "You're too light for a freight engine, a heavy Mogul, but you might be able to handle a passenger engine. Nick, here's your fireman. He'll help you pull the invalids to Richfield Springs. If he gets you stuck in a cow pasture, God help him."

The scrawny little man, to whom Old Tom had turned me over with such lack of enthusiasm, nodded, and I followed him into the yard.

"I'm Nick Kuhn. What's your name, son? I guess you haven't been firing very long, but we've got a sweet little engine and she won't give you any trouble. We pull out at 12:45, and I'll meet you at the roundhouse."

After an early dinner, I went back with my overalls in a black pasteboard suitcase, put them on in a corner of the roundhouse and met Nick at the ready track. The air was full of cinders, and there was the sharp, sticky smell of coal, more acid than wood. She was a handsome engine, light and delicate as a lady, with high runners and the lettering on her cab in gold leaf shaded with blue. On her front was mounted a pair of antlers that Nick said belonged to a stag he had shot on Panther Mountain. The conductor handed up the orders, we tied onto our train (a couple of coaches and a combo) and eased into the station.

"We pull the swells," Nick told me. "Wait until we pick up the Wagner drawing-room from New York at Richfield Junction—six hundred dollars' worth of gilt curlicues and gimcracks in that one car. Ever been to the Springs?" I shook my head. "It's higher than Saratoga and prettier, the sulphur water tastes just as awful and you can lose your shirt on the nags as easily one place as another."

There was a bed of red coals in the firebox, an enormous long one that stretched back eleven feet; and when I looked at the gauge, I noticed that the pop valve was spouting a white feather. The needle was almost on the line, so I opened the door and threw in a load of coal— hard coal, in lumps as big as a man's head, that were difficult to keep on the scoop. Pulling my bandanna over my chin to protect it from the blistering heat, I threw in a generous layer, then slammed the door and glanced at Nick, who was watching me dubiously. But he didn't say anything. We coasted into New Hartford and hadn't used much steam; but at Washington Mills we began to climb, and the gauge was falling lower and lower. I opened the door and saw that what had been a clear red fire was a smoldering hump of half-burned coals. The fire was going out! Franticly I punched it with the slash bar, trying to open it up for air.

"You ain't never fired coal, have you, son?" Nick

climbed down off the driver's seat and peered into the furnace. He motioned to me, and we both looked inside.

"You see, when the engine's running, the coal hops to the front and fills up so thick it smothers itself. Every time the exhaust lets out a blast, it takes another hop front. Now, here's the trick." He picked up the clinker hook and spread the coal to the sides and back, leaving a low bed of red coals in the middle. Giving the grate a mighty shake, he slammed the door shut and climbed back on his seat.

"Don't you worry now, she'll come up in a minute. Then put a little in on the back corners. Always leave your middle low." I tried again, but somehow I had ruined the good fire with which we had started. When we got to Richfield Junction, we were four minutes late; but we still had a minute to clear into the switch and wait for our meet with the highball, the fast train from Binghamton that carried the New York drawing-room.

Nick told me to shake down the grate and dump the ash pan and be sure to put out the cinders. I shook with all my might, and when we came to a dead stop, I climbed under the front wheels to get at the pan. A brakeman was protecting, but it was nervous work with a live engine over me. Crawling out, I drew a great breath as if my lungs would burst, feeling like a squirrel that had wriggled free of a trap.

Gently we tied into the drawing-room and switched over onto the fifty-mile road that ran to the Springs. We were out of the Mohawk Valley now and climbing into hills with lakes in their high depressions and farms with cattle grazing right up to the tracks. You could almost lean out of the window and tinkle the bells around the necks of the sleek, indifferent cows.

But I had no eye for all this beauty. I was nursing the fire, watching the lazy indicator and the gauge, on which there was no sign of a plume of steam. Nick opened the door and looked in.

"That's better, lots better. Just remember to fire when she's about to pop and rake when she goes down. You'll get onto it." But I doubted if I ever would. Waiting for the coals to burn out, I stood by the window and watched the hills march past, too discouraged to meet the runner's eye. At East Winfield, when we stopped for a flag, the conductor came ahead with his watch in his hand.

"What's the matter, Nick? Having trouble? We're three minutes late."

Nick grinned at him. "Go on back and plant yourself on a cushion. We'll make it all right."

We got the highball and picked up as fast as we could.

"Don't let that big ox get you down, kid," Nick said.

I opened the door and spread a little coal in the back corners and loosened up a pile of clinkers. The glow in the middle was a little whiter, but not much, and I felt miserable and small enough to poke myself through the holes in the grate. Then I looked out, just as Nick tooted for Cedarville Crossing, and there was a girl standing on tip-toe waiting for the train to pass—a young girl in a blue gingham dress with a sunbonnet in her hand and two long yellow plaits hanging to her waist. She looked up at the engine, and her eyes were so eager and blue, so full of the glamor of places she had never seen, that my pride came back.

"Hello," I called. She waved her sunbonnet, and I looked back until we screeched around a curve. I opened the fire door and gave the coals a mighty rake. The pointer began to climb, and we shot into Richfield Springs only one minute behind the schedule. By the time we got back to Utica, I had the hang of the thing and didn't do so badly. The Old Man stamped out of his office as we wheeled into the roundhouse.

"So you stabbed the highball at the Junction. Did this Black River strong man let the fire go out?"

"We didn't hold her up," Nick protested. "We had a minute to clear, and Joe's doing fine."

On the next trip we kept to the schedule, and by the time we came in sight of Cedarville Crossing, we were running with a full head of steam. There was the girl again, leaning against a fence. Every day she was there, sometimes even in the rain, looking up and laughing, with the water dripping from the brim of a man's old campaign hat. One day I dropped a note wrapped around a sliver of coal, and asked her name. "Rose," she called. At least, that was what it sounded like above the pounding of the runners.

Sometimes I tossed out magazines, which the shack gave me when he found them in the drawing-room before old Hopsky, the newsboy, could gather them up and sell them again. She threw me peaches that she carried in her bonnet. When I caught them, I gave them to Nick, bribing him to slow down; but oftener than not they smashed against the jacket of his precious engine, and I had to clean them off.

Had she ever been to Richfield Springs, I asked in another note; and the next afternoon she shook her head. Nick saw that I was brooding over something as I sat abstractedly on my box, waiting to rake or fire, and asked me what was on my mind. I was wrestling with an idea—the idea of picking up little Rose on this snorting chariot, that she thought so wonderful, and taking her to the Springs to see the fashionable world. But the harder I thought about it, the more impossible it seemed. Nick, I felt sure, would not let her ride on his engine; and I didn't have the money to buy her a ticket. It was a week until payday, and the best I could manage was a dollar to spend on her at the Springs.

Nick polished the face of his fat gold watch with his thumb, in a way he had when he was struggling with a thought. Well, why not take her on the engine? he decided. A kid is only young once; and besides, he thought she was a pretty little morsel. He'd tell the big ox to make a flag stop at the crossing. Every day the conductor watched for Rose, and he was a sentimental old dodo with a nose for romance. We could bring her back on our return trip at five o'clock, and that would give Rose and me two hours to see the town. I had twinges of worry, because if anything went wrong and the Old Man heard about it, he might put the finger on us. But Nick slapped me on the back and said it would do him and the big ox good to take a chance—make them feel frisky and young again.

I tossed a note to Rose, and on a clear, warm September day, so blue and still that you couldn't tell the sky from the lakes, Nick stopped the train neatly, with the cab

directly on the crossing. I pulled up Rose, and the conductor waved us on, all in the same breath. Here she was, so close that I could touch her, in a ruffled blue dress that billowed about her ankles and a straw bonnet tied under the chin. I dusted my seat for her, but she was too eager to sit still, and wanted to watch Nick and know about everything. Blown up with pride like a pouter pigeon, he let her put her hand under his on the throttle and the lever. Then she came over to my side and looked into the furnace when I fired. She stuck her head out of the cab window to cool her cheeks, laughing, with yellow wisps of hair curling loose under the bonnet. And her voice was clear and light, the way I had thought I heard it when she called to me above the thunder of the runners.

At Richfield Springs the head brakeman offered to dump my fire and clean the grate. Rose waited in the cab while I shed my overalls in a corner of the roundhouse. Then I held up my arms and she jumped to the track. Smoothing down her ruffles, she called to Nick, "Thank you. It was a lovely ride."

"Well, Miss Rose," he answered, "you sure do sling a wicked peach. The best I ever ate. Now don't let Joe here make you late for the 5:16."

We thanked him and walked up the street, Rose holding tight to my hand like a little girl. We passed the American House, with its long portico and white pillars three stories high; and went on to the Spring House, set in its own exclusive park. In front of it a big double-decked tallyho drawn by six horses was filling up for a trip to the head of the lake. Rose stood entranced, looking at the red panels on the coach, the shining brass on the harness of the horses and the flowered bonnets of the women sitting atop, pointing their tiny ruffled parasols at the sun. When it had rolled out of sight, we walked past the Spring House park and looked over the fence at young men in knee breeches and peaked baseball caps batting tennis balls to girls, who ran after them awkwardly in their long looped and ruffled skirts.

At a shop near the waterfall I bought a bag of little cakes with icing and walnuts on them, two bottles of pop, and a bag of peanuts; and we carried them to a bench and watched the riders canter past on the bridle path. The bobtailed horses were sleek and lively, arching their necks and lifting their dainty feet. They swept by, four or five abreast, the red coats and light breeches of the men bright against the sober riding skirts of the women.

Rose drank her pop with solemn rapture. "They're so beautiful, Joe," she said, letting the chocolate icing from the cake fall on her clean blue dress. "Everything is so beautiful!"

I took my handkerchief and tried to get out the stain, afraid her mother would scold—if she had a mother. We hadn't bothered to tell each other about ourselves, we were Rose and Joe as if we had known each other always.

She watched proudly when I looked at my new gold watch, as big as a turnip, that I was buying on the instalment plan. It was time to go, so we walked back along another street lined with the elegant houses of the summer people, set in lawns as smooth as the palm of your hand. Out of the drives rolled carriages with footmen and coachmen and pretty women in flowered bonnets; and on the walk we passed starched and ruffled children hanging onto their nurses' hands. Rose stepped lightly, as if she were walking in fairyland.

Near the station was a shop with a window full of little china boxes decorated with pictures of the Springs, hatpins made of Indian arrowheads, and all sorts of souvenirs. I still had part of my dollar and wanted to give Rose a present so that she would never forget our afternoon. She put her face close to the window, looked for a long time before she could make up her mind, and finally chose a fan with a picture of a tallyho with high red wheels and a coachman in a yellow hat. It took all of my money but a nickel, and that I spent on a package of chewing-gum, to give her on the train. I wanted to give her everything I had, for she was my sweetheart, my little yellow-haired sweetheart. That was the way I thought about her, although I would have choked if I had tried to tell her so.

Nick was at the station waiting for us. He helped Rose into the cab, and she sat on my seat, leaning against the wall, nodding under her bonnet, exhausted with too many wonders. As Nick slowed down for the crossing, I touched her shoulder, and she looked up with sleepy eyes.

"Here you are. Will it be all right with your folks?" Nick asked anxiously.

"Oh, I 'spect I'll get a whipping," Rose said, awake now and smiling, "but I've had the loveliest time in all my life. Good-by," she called when we dropped her to the road. "Good-by, and don't forget me, Joe."

The next day I had a note ready for Rose, but she wasn't at the crossing. The day after, it rained so hard that no one was on the roads, and we couldn't see more than a foot ahead. When we got back to Utica, the Old Man had put me on a local freight to Binghamton. The season at the Springs was over, the fast train was cut off and the drawing-room to New York. Nick was put on a passenger run, and I didn't see him often. For months I grieved for Rose, my little sweetheart at Cedarville Crossing, wishing I could write her or send her a message; but I didn't even know her name.

6. Boomers on the Coal

HAULING COAL IS A LOT TOUGHER THAN pulling around a string of plush. Think you can keep up the steam?"

"Sure," I told the Old Man, "I can keep steam for any load you can tie to the engine."

"Don't be so damned sure," he snorted, waggling his whiskers. "Boney Young will take you out."

Later, in the yard, when Nick Kuhn asked me who was my engineer, I understood why the Old Man had grinned.

"Boney's a hog for power," Nick told me. "He keeps the lever down in the corner with the oil cans. Oh, boy, will you spend your evening soaking your hams in oil."

At seven o'clock on a frosty November morning, the caller thumped on the door and ordered me out for eight-fifteen. The coal trains were not on schedule. Whenever a train was ready to move north, the Binghamton office wired Utica, and we started after it at any hour, day or night. Eight or nine coal trains a day wildcatted over the division, hauling anthracite from Pennsylvania: rice, buckwheat, egg, stove, and lump coal for the Erie Canal, the Hudson, and tidewater. What with time lost holing up for fast freights and passengers and doubling up Paris Hill, we counted on twelve hours each way; so mother packed my lunch pail with food for a couple of days.

Hurrying to the yard, I looked over the engine, checked the fire and water and dusted around before Boney Young came ambling over to the ready track—a tall thin man, all angles, with a clean-shaven face as tough as saddle leather, and across his chest a watch chain that would have anchored a battleship. Boney climbed into the cab, let out a puff of steam and looked me over; but while we tied on our empties, he never said a word except, "Good morning, kid." As we pulled out across the drawbridge over the canal, he spat a neat stream of tobacco juice at the locks, closed now for the winter, and turned his attention to me. Ears burning, conscious of my skimpy frame, I felt that he was not too enthusiastic about his helper.

"Where'd you come from?" he asked me, and I told him a farm up Ithaca way.

"Boy," he said, "you look it."

You couldn't talk back to your engineer. Hot-eyed, I stared out of my window as we bumped along Schuyler Street and slowed for the signalman's "go ahead" at the New York, Ontario & Western crossing. As we pulled out of the Mohawk Valley, past the little mill towns that made shoes and cotton, silk and plows and woollens in the midst of woods and dairy farms, I chucked a lump or two into the rat-hole, while Boney looked at the scenery and sang *Beulah Land*. It was a sparkling morning, the frost gleamed on the pasture grass, and the maples and scrub oaks were yellow and crimson in the pine woods. The engine steamed sweetly, pulling the empties up the grade as if she had nothing on her tail. Boney sang at the top of a loud and foggy voice.

After we left Richfield Junction and were still climbing toward Paris, Boney questioned me again.

"How long you been firing, kid?"

"Three months," I answered, and added that I intended to stick until I was set up with an engine of my own.

"It takes brains to be an engineer, boy." Letting out the throttle to lift us over the hump, he considered me with a detached and not unfriendly eye.

"You might be able to make it," he concluded, "but I doubt it."

We were too busy at Paris for me to resent the old man's words. Here at the summit of the ridge were long switches filled with empties, gondolas for Binghamton, and "jimmies" (old-fashioned coal cars with tall hand brakes at the sides). We tied on all of them that the conductor thought we could drag. Our "brains," Gander Schnell, came back to talk to Boney while we were switching, and I saw the famous Adam's apple that, according to the legend in the yards, bobbed up and down when he was angry, like a monkey on a string.

"Boy, what is the difference between a stock car and a conductor?" Boney shot at me when Gander went back to look at his wheels. I shook my head, although it was an old joke: one was a car for hogs, and the other a hog for cars. He told it with gusto and added, "That's Gander, all right. Bet you we drag eighty or ninety cars."

But the load didn't worry Boney. We shot down Paris Hill, the empties dancing like a line of drunken sailors.

They settled down when we hit the Brookfield swamp, where there was nine miles of the straightest track on the road. The right of way ran along the east side of the long, narrow valley, and out of Boney's window I could see the Chenango River, not slow and muddy like the Mohawk, but swift water, clear and gleaming, with now and then a pool of backwater, dark with fallen leaves. Along the bank were farms carved out of tall woods that had never been touched by an ax.

"Pretty, ain't it?" said Boney, leaning out to look at the mistletoe and scarlet bittersweet that hung from the trees. "Boy, I've roared down the Iron Mountain, and I've run drags of coal along the New River, the prettiest sight in the Blue Ridge, and I've stoked passengers on the S.P., but I've never seen a spot as nice as this. If it was in the old country, we'd be running excursions to look at it."

Boney Young was a boomer; he had the itching feet, always moving on to somewhere new, looking for better times. As we roared through Pooleville, where a small lake, as blue and clear as mother's rinse-water on washing day, came up and lapped at the track, he told me tales of the high iron—especially of the Pacific Coast, where he had pulled a string of sleepers the year before. He was firing a Mallett, and, like all of these powerful drivers, she leaked at the flues; so they were always running in a cloud of steam. The eagle-eye kept a bag of flour and made Boney put a little of it in the tank to plug the leaks. When the engine hit a grade and the draft was strong, the oil from the cylinder mixed with the flour, and gobs of it flew out of the stack, baked as hard as bread from an oven.

"And they were cooked so well," Boney said, looking me straight in the eye, "that when the chef ran short of bread, he hung off the diner steps, caught the hunks of dough in a skillet and served them for biscuits."

At the next station we crossed the old Chenango Canal and followed it into the valley. It had been abandoned for years, ever since the railroad hauled the coal, and was filled with rushes and cattails as high as a man's head. Sometimes we lost it, where the farmers had filled it up or dammed it to make a pool of storage water for the cattle. Now I had to fire more steadily, for it took power to snake the drag around curves. The railroad followed the river, which twisted through the hills, first on one side of us, then the other.

"Reckon they decided curves were cheaper than bridges," Boney sighed, "but they never counted the wear and tear on their engineers." There was no chance for an eagle-eye to nap on a reverse curve.

At Norwich, where we had to stop for orders and hole up for a through passenger, I ate my lunch in the tender; and Boney went over to the railroad restaurant for a dinner "on tick" from the white-whiskered old counterman whom he called "Santa Claus." Gander Schnell clucked us together the minute the string of plush cleared the station. Boney muttered that Gander wanted to get to Binghamton in time for a date with a widow who set him up to an elegant cherry pie.

We rattled along with a clear track until we passed Brisben and stopped for water on a curve that swept around the river in an almost perfect horseshoe—Grecian

Bend, the trainmen called it. At the head was a water tank for freights and coal trains. While Boney oiled around, I pulled a few clinkers out of my firebox and leaned out of the window. It was late afternoon, the shadows of the trees along the bank criss-crossed the two lanes of water with rippling patterns and the string of empties on our tail shimmied in the river. The head brakie called "OK," climbed back into the tender, and Boney eased out the throttle while he shouted to the forests the praises of his eternal *Beulah Land*.

After we passed Chenango Forks and cleared the junction with the Syracuse Branch, which ran with us into the city, Boney asked me if I had ever been to Binghamton. When I admitted that this was my first trip, he wrinkled his leathery forehead.

"Where are you going to pound your ear, kid?"

"Mother thought perhaps I could go with you, Mr. Young," I answered, polite as I knew how.

Boney shook his head. "Kid, I'm as free from money as a turtle is from feathers. I ran against a full house with a flush last night, and I've nothing between me and the day the ghost walks but a pie card with old Santa Claus. Now, if you have two bits, you can go over to the Grove Hotel, get the key to the Utica room from Dennis, and I'll meet you at the side door. We'll be gone in the morning before he opens up."

I didn't understand about the Utica room and Dennis and the side door, but I didn't have to display my ignorance.

"Mr. Young," I told him, "I'm free from feathers, too."

"Never mind, kid, we'll get along." After we had turned the empties over to the yard goats and run the engine into the roundhouse, Boney told me to get the cushions from the cab and leave a call for the McKinney House. I followed him across the tracks to a coal yard with "McKinney" painted on the office shack. We climbed a high ladder to a dumping shed on a trestle and scrambled over the cars waiting to be unloaded. Finally Boney reached one filled with rice coal.

"It fits your body like a feather bed," he said.

After we had settled ourselves, Boney asked me what was left in my dinner pail. I opened it. We ate mother's sandwiches and pie to the last bite and faced the next day without a crumb or a nickel between us. My mind was crowded with misgivings, but Boney was untroubled. After a few bars of *Beulah Land*, he rooted into the coal and began to snore.

My arms ached, and one of my thumbs smarted where I had broken a water blister, but I didn't lie awake long listening to the noises in the dark. At daylight I was roused by a mighty twittering and saw that we were not the only guests of the McKinney House. The cross-beams of the shed were the roosts of a flock of sparrows. I looked over at Boney, snoring peacefully on his back, and noticed that his overalls were covered with white specks, which made them look like a suit of pepper-and-salt. So did mine. As I stood up to clean myself, Boney opened his eyes.

"Never mind, kid," he said. "It's just the sparrows' calling-cards. Wait till it dries, and it will brush right off." He turned over on his ear, and I lay down again, listening to the ducks gabbling in the pond behind the enginehouse and the yard goats shoving the cars around.

We were a long time tying on our load of sixty jimmies. The brakemen hated these old cars with their awkward brakes; they were always coming uncoupled, running away or killing a man. The eagle-eye had to crawl along with them at twelve miles an hour, under the threat of a flock of "Brownies" if he speeded up above fifteen. "Brownies"—demerits—were named for the man who invented the system, which called for so many black marks, so many days off without pay. Consequently, we had no liking for Mr. Brown.

By the time we clanked out of the yards, I was too empty to look at Binghamton by daylight, although Boney said it was called the "parlor city" because the front yards were as neat and well kept as a New England front room. When we stopped for water at the Grecian Bend, my ribs were sticking together. For a long time I hesitated to say anything to Boney, who was as cheerful as a robin with a worm; but finally I asked, "When do we eat?"

"Poor kid. Hang on until we get to Norwich. I'll wire old Santa Claus to bring us each a pail of hotcakes and coffee, ham and eggs, and a piece of pie." He let out the throttle, and the engine played crack-the-whip with the jimmies as we lurched around the curves.

Old Santa Claus was waiting for us with the pails. Fortified with ham and eggs and a quarter of an apple pie, I settled down to the business of keeping up the fire. No time to look out the window now and watch the cattle drinking in the canal; it took all the power the engine had to drag a heavy load of coal along a road as crooked as a wiggling snake. Boney pulled the lever to the floor, looked over at me and grinned.

"Boy, you don't know what firing is till you come to Paris Hill. There's where the Lackawanna teaches her men to cuss."

We spent so much time holing up on a siding at Pooleville that it was already twilight when we charged into the straight track through Brookfield swamp. Boney sat back, easing up for a good run, and began to warble. Suddenly he leaned forward and stopped in the middle of a bar, peered down the track and shut off the steam. I looked but could see nothing in the headlight, which fanned out wanly in the dusk.

"What's the matter, Mr. Young?" I asked.

Boney hesitated and answered sheepishly, "I thought I saw a black cat run across the track. I don't believe in them, boy, but I don't want any accident." He kept the throttle in and hung out the window, but a moment later he pulled back his nose, just as mine connected with a powerful stink.

"Praise the Lord, kid, it wasn't a black cat. I wouldn't sleep for a month if I ran over one. Guess we're lucky God didn't make a skunk as big as a cow."

After we had passed through the worst of the odor, Boney told me to stick out my beak and see if Gander was signalling for speed.

"One of the best things about pulling freight is, your conductor can't sit in the hind end and hound you with a whistle," he told me, running his hand complacently over his bald head. "Ever since old Pappy Ayres on the Erie got tired of climbing up on his tail car and getting frostbite signalling the smoky end, the conductors of the passengers have had the edge on the eagle-eyes. Pappy strung a cord from his hind car to the engine, with a chunk of wood tied to the front end, and made a devil of a clatter jerking it. That piece of wood was the grand-daddy of the conductor's whistle on the passenger. It sure did tie the runner down. You could always say you didn't see the old arm signal, but you can't say you're deaf and get by with the Supe."

Boney grinned and pulled out the throttle. The train picked up speed: twelve, fourteen miles, nearly fifteen. While I hacked at a lump of coal too large to get through the firebox door, I heard the gritting of sand and saw Boney pull on the brake, heard the wheels scream as they slid on the rails, and pitched forward, landing against the firebox door. Straightening up, I looked through the front window to see the figure of a woman shoot up into the glare of the headlight. Making a wide curve through the air, she settled on the bank at the side of the road.

While the engine was still quivering, Boney dropped down the handrail, and I followed. Spattered on the pilot were the remains of two horses, and the kindling-wood that had been a wagon was scattered along the right of way. Rattling with fright, Boney crossed to the woman and bent over to see what was left of her. The bundle moved, the woman sat up, rubbed her eyes and climbed to her feet.

"Oh," she groaned, rubbing her thigh, "I got an awful

bump." Looking around, she saw the dead horses and the wrecked wagon and began to cry. "Wait until my father hears of this," she sobbed. "You're murderers, just plain murderers, this railroad!"

The head brakie had climbed out of the tender with a lantern, and Gander Schnell was coming up the track picking the gravel out of his face. He was so angry that he could do no more than splutter, and my fascinated eyes clung to the Adam's apple bobbing in his throat. But when he saw what had happened, he was all solicitude. He insisted that Boney and the head shack take the lantern and see the woman home to the farmhouse, which was a quarter of a mile down the woods path (scarcely more than a couple of wheel tracks) that she had been following when she crossed the rails. When they had disappeared into the woods, and we could no longer hear her voice berating the men, we went back to see what damage the train had suffered.

Luckily the jimmies were on the rails, but the front end of the caboose was bashed in and the hind brakie was dancing up and down in pain. He had been cooking a stolen chicken in the coal bucket and, when the jolt came, had tried to stop the red-hot stove as it bounded toward the door. Gander Schnell and the second brakie were able to pin the coupling together; so Gander sent two men to protect the ends with a drumstick in one hand, fusees and lanterns in the other, while we oiled the hind brake's hands. Waiting for Boney, we gloomily ate the rest of the chicken.

After a while I went to the engine to look at the fire

and saw Boney's lantern bobbing through the woods. Below the cab I could hear him and Gander muttering together.

"The Supe will be plenty riled," Gander warned. "Ain't nothing he likes less than a farmer spouting brimstone with a warrant in his hand."

Boney groaned. "You know very well it ain't a regular crossing."

He climbed on, whistled in the shacks and we picked up speed, but he was subdued, hunched silently in his corner. When we reached Paris Hill and had to double, thirty cars at a time, he growled at the engine—a good steamer but she slipped with a heavy load; and he snapped when I left the fire door open for longer than a second. The hook for poking the fire was red-hot, the whole sixteen feet of it, to within a foot of my blistered hands.

Finally we slid down into the valley, and Boney told me to sign in and clear out quickly before the Old Man started to curse about the broken caboose. I scooted out of the yard as fast as I could, but the boys told me that Old Tom was hot enough to bust a boiler. That night mother put cold, wet cloths on my smarting eyes and soaked my hands in oil.

"Joe, I was right," Boney told me solemnly, when we pulled out in the morning. "Skunk or no skunk, I did see a black cat in the swamp. That was why it happened." Nothing would shake him from his superstition.

But no misfortune overtook Boney because of the accident. He was cleared of responsibility, and we were relieved, for we were all fond of him. In spite of his rough ways, Boney was a fine man. On Sundays he dressed in his best black suit and went to church whenever he could get there. He could and did quote the Bible from beginning to end, and never cursed unless he was hopping mad. He had always followed the railroad. The first thing he could remember was standing at the foot of a lookout post beside a little way station in Pennsylvania and bawling because his father wouldn't let him climb it. The stationmasters in those days climbed the thirty-foot mast with a spy-glass around their neck and watched for the trains.

When the Pennsylvania added a gallows arm to the top of the mast and hung a ball on it, which was raised and lowered by a rope, Boney had pulled it up and down, working one of the first ball signals on the railroads. His father, clinging to the top of the mast, with his spyglass steadied against the gallows arm and his trousers flapping against his chilly shanks, called down to Boney, "Number 7 is in sight," and up went the white ball to the top. If there were passengers or freight for Number 7, Boney left the ball at half-mast.

"That was where you get your highball and lowball signals," Boney told me. "At night we signalled with candles in the station window. But Pop had it easy. My uncle, who was stationmaster on the Boston & Maine, had to ride a horse down the tracks when the trains were an hour late and see what had happened to them. Many's the time I have seen him come back with his breath frozen to his whiskers."

The very thought of such rigors made Boney shiver.

He was no polar bear, and I could see that he was getting restless for Florida.

"Better come with me, Joe, and take a look around the country," he said; but eager as I was to go, there was my mother to think of, and I knew that I was doomed to stay with the home guard. Enviously I saw Boney off, deadheading on a fast freight for New York.

"Good-by, Joe," he called, hanging his lanky frame out of the caboose window, "good-by. I'll send you an alligator."

7. The Overalls Hop

T HE OLD MAN CURSED ALL BOOMERS AS good-for-nothing tramps, but he was short-handed and couldn't do without them. This was the season when the "woodchucks" who didn't like to go out in bad weather filled the "laid off" corner of the call board with their name-pegs; so the Old Man had no choice but to send out with our crew another boomer who had drifted in from the Iron Mountain road.

Most boomers were single men and travelled light; but Henry Millgate was encumbered with a wife, seven children, and a mongrel terrier named Bosto. Henry was a long-legged fellow, so tall that he couldn't stand up straight in the cab; and he had a round, good-natured face behind a fringe of choppy red whiskers set unexpectedly on a flagpole of a neck. On his first trip, I learned all about his family, especially his beautiful daughter, Sarah, who (he promised) would give me a cordial welcome if I came around to see her; but the other firemen hooted at Henry's description of her and maintained that Sarah looked like a bag of feed with a string around the middle.

Henry was a good man and an optimist. He knew his Bible and he never drank, swore, or chewed—or paid his debts. Everything, he believed, worked out for the best if looked at in the right way. With simple faith, he expected manna from Heaven, and Heaven provided it, on the Installment plan. The more installments he evaded, the more prosperous he felt.

One of Henry's first installment purchases was a clock —costly and handsome, according to his description. It rang the quarter and half hours, with a full-length melody on the hour. The oldest boy wanted to make it play longer, so he took it apart; but when he tried to put it together, he left out several of the wheels. Henry didn't mind. He said the boy was smart to get it together at all, and besides, he never had liked the tune.

One morning he climbed on the engine, let off a playful jet of steam to frighten a cat, and told me with a broad smile spreading his whiskers that he had bought a house. He pointed it out on Schuyler Street, as we rolled by, and waved proudly to the little Millgates swarming in the yard.

"It's good business, Joe. I'm tired of being a sucker and paying rent. This only costs me five dollars a month," he boasted. Perhaps he intended to pay the five dollars, but he never got around to it. Almost every morning an installment agent was waiting for the genial Henry by the "ready" track.

"Good morning, Mr. Aaronson, fine morning," Henry would greet his creditor, with a beaming smile.

"Good morning, Mr. Millgate. How about a little money on that installment this morning?"

"So sorry, Mr. Aaronson, I've got to pull out this drag,

but I'll have it for you. Don't you worry. Good-by. See you soon." With a flourish he waved to the discouraged collector, let out the throttle and rolled out of the yard, pleased with himself all morning for the nonchalant way in which he had carried off the encounter.

Not long after he bought the house, Henry told me he had his eye on a horse: he was sick and tired of paying money out to street cars. Gander Schnell, who had grown up on a farm, asked derisively about the steed's points, and the shacks tried to josh Henry; but he was too pleased with himself to be annoyed. Nothing bothered him, not even getting stuck on Paris Hill and spending an hour coaxing the engine to make the grade. By that time I didn't mind it either, for my hands were tough as rawhide and I could manage the fire without blistering them with the red-hot poker.

The day the horse came, Henry tooted as we ran through Schuyler Street, and one of the boys brought the nag out to the front yard to show her off—a broken-down strawberry roan with a hang-dog look and a white spot in one eye.

"Well," said Gander, "she *is* a horse. You wouldn't mistake her for a goat." From that day, Henry concentrated on building a shed to house the animal. Every time we shunted around the yard, he kept his eye out for loose planks.

"There's one now!" he would shout, and leap off to pile it on the tank. When we ran by the house, he tossed off the boards, and the children pulled them into the yard.

Henry's next problem was feed. He decided to give his

patronage to a dealer in Sherburne, who had a store directly across from the tracks—a nice fellow, who always spoke to him every time we holed up on the siding. Henry bought a bag of bran and put it in an empty boxcar that was tied on with the gondolas. At Norwich he announced that he intended to give the rest of his business to Sloan Feed & Hay, a firm with a big sign that was one of the landmarks of the road; so he bought a bale of hay and put it in the same car with the bran. Gander Schnell was amused by Henry's air of big business and didn't mention until we had passed Oxford that the boxcar was to be thrown out at the next station. For a moment Henry suspected that Gander was playing a trick on him; but the hind brakeman said it was true, and suggested that he leave the feed on the platform and pick it up on the return trip.

Next day we were dragging twenty gondolas of coal, and the only place for Henry's merchandise was on the pilot sticking out in front of the engine. He tied on the bran and hay with bell cord and said it was just as well, for he could keep an eye on them. Going up Paris Hill, I built up the fire, and Henry put the lever down in the corner. As the sparks flew from the stack, Henry thrust his head out the window.

"I do declare," he shouted, "the hay's afire."

He leaped out with a pail of water and doused the hay as he ran alongside; but by the time we reached the top of the hill, it was roaring, and the bran had caught. They were both charred ruins, and Henry had to kick them off and leave them beside the track.

Even Gander was sorry and came front to help, but

Henry was not discouraged. He climbed back into the cab, wiped his hands on a piece of waste and said cheerily, "I don't believe that feed was very good, anyway. Next time I'll buy my stuff at home."

Henry stayed on in Schuyler Street for a couple of seasons, a long time for a boomer. He stayed until he was put out of the house and had exhausted all of the installment companies. Then he told us that his health was about to crack in this unholy climate and he had to go to California for a rest.

We didn't have vacations in those days, except the ones without pay that we gave ourselves, or lay-offs imposed by the Old Man for rough handling and "pulling a lung" or losing a hind end. As mother could barely get along, I never lost a day. Sometimes in the late summer when the hops were ripe in the lush valleys around Brookfield, I wished I could go hopping for a couple of weeks. Almost every farm between Norwich and Paris Hill had a hop yard, some of them close along the tracks. Whole families from Utica and Binghamton and the villages along the Chenango swarmed into the district, camped in the farmers' improvised dormitories, ate the farmers' good hog meat and vegetables and fattened the children on fresh milk with the foam still on it. Sometimes the Lackawanna put on special trains to handle the crowds, and almost every passenger that scooted by us had an extra coach on its tail.

But the young sports who went hopping for adventure preferred to ride the rods. They generally picked the coal trains, and for a few days before the beginning of the season Henry and I counted as many as two hundred free-trippers on a single drag. They made themselves comfortable on the coal, well back toward the caboose, out of range of the sparks from the smokestack, which sprayed the first ten or twelve cars. The crew was helpless in the face of numbers; so the road made no attempt to throw them off. Gander Schnell even called out "Brookfield" when we neared the town, to keep them from setting the brakes, as they often did when they thought that they were being carried too far.

The boys slept in the hay barns in the meadows and lived on pig potatoes and corn, which they bought, careful not to steal or play any pranks that would gain them the ill-will of the farmers. Fishing in the Chenango, dancing and singing at night to the music of a jews'-harp or a homemade fiddle, flirting with the girls, and games of poker in the straw by lantern light, all made the work seem like play.

One of the Binghamton boys who never failed to go hop-picking was Bishop Coleman, who lived just across the tracks from the yard. His father, a wiper in the roundhouse who often took care of my engine, told me how Bish had lost his leg when he was a boy, trying to jump a "rattler." A happy soul, lazy and a little too fond of booze, Bish played on everybody's sympathy with his appealing smile.

All spring Bish spent making a pegleg from the trunk of a golden willow that he had seasoned for over a year—whittling away at it, intent on getting it smoothed and properly tapered before the hop-picking began. I asked the mechanic in the shop for a brass ring to put over the end, so that it wouldn't wear away, and helped him fit the socket. It worked well, except when he was shooting craps. Sitting on his good leg and bending over to roll the dice, he swung his wooden leg in an arc that was a menace to the rest of the players, unless they were quick to leap out of the way.

When the hopping season opened, I cautioned Bish to look out for my drag. Henry's Sarah and the oldest boy were picking near Waterville, so I knew Henry would be sympathetic and hold the train long enough for the boy to climb on. It wouldn't do for Bish to run the risk of smashing either his good leg or his wooden one.

We deposited the hoppers at Brookfield or Hubbardsville. Every day, when we went by, I hung out the window, remembering the summers when mother took me hopping and I played hide-and-seek with the other children among the hop boxes (which were ten feet long and taller than a boy's head). From the train I could see the bright sunbonnets, pink and blue and violet, above the boxes with the hop poles laid across them; and farther down the hills, the poles that were not yet gathered, standing twice the height of a man, with yellow hops among the leaves.

"Hop pole," we boys used to shout, mimicking the hoppers, and tagging after the pole-puller, who brought unpicked vines and took away the stripped poles; or "Hop sack," when a box was full. Then the foreman gave the picker a ticket, stuffed the box-load into a sack and dumped it into the wagon, which a sleepy horse pulled between the rows. Although we didn't know what all the fuss was about, we laughed and shouted with the grown-ups when a girl found a "kissing ring," a vine that had made a complete loop and was growing back upon itself. She was privileged to kiss the boy of her choice.

Every day, as we went by, I waved to the pickers and envied Bish and his friends. At the end of the season they came home burned as tan as Indians, riding on the plush with money jingling in their pockets. Even Henry's Sarah returned with color in her cheeks and a visible waistline.

Once I asked Henry if he didn't think it would be more fun walking up and down the hop rows than running the engine. He looked at me in incredulous distaste.

"Heavens, no," he said. "I never did like to sleep in the hay. It tickles my neck."

Although we didn't pick hops, we railroaders had plenty of good times, with dances on Saturday nights, and hunting or fishing on Sundays. In summer we went to the tent shows, "East Lynne" and "Uncle Tom's Cabin," threw peanuts at the girls and drank pop from the bottle, while we watched Little Eva, miraculously resurrected from the tent tops, selling postcards in the audience. And when we saw that the angel child was a plump little blonde who would never see her 'teens again, we ogled her and tried to date her for a glass of beer after the performance.

On almost any summer evening we could find a medicine show in one of the vacant lots downtown: the white man who came around each season dressed as an Indian, selling bottles of "Kickaboo," good for any ailment of man or beast; or the dentist who drove two white ponies through the streets and put on a fine vaudeville show on a platform under a red velvet canopy, pulling teeth for fifty cents a yank. My favorite was the seller of "Tigemar," a little jar of cream that looked like lard and was purported to be the marrow from a tiger's rib. The medicine man had discovered the secret while hunting with an Indian maharajah. The wicked beast had disemboweled one of the beaters; the maharajah slew the tiger; a slave cracked one of its ribs and applied the marrow to the dying man. In a day he was healed, in two days he was hunting again. Never could the medicine man rest until he had combined the tiger's marrow with our fine native New England herbs and given to the world this marvelous remedy.

Then there were the hole-in-the-wall shows, such as the perpetual motion machine of Professor Michael O'Grady, which came, stayed until it exhausted our credulity and moved on to newer territory. Tad Millgate (one of Henry's smaller boys) and I were standing idly on the corner of Bleecker Street looking for amusement when we first clapped eyes on the professor, standing on the sidewalk in front of a vacant store, barking the wonders of his machine. His elegance was dumbfounding: pearl gray high hat, mustache waxed to a needle point, a tight-fitting frock coat and striped trousers, patent leather shoes with pearl buttons, a gold-headed cane, and a manner that topped them all.

With his cane the professor pointed out a large lithograph in the window. I edged up and read about the wonders of the machine, which had been invented by a famous London shipbuilder, who willed it to the British Museum,

from which the professor had rented it at a great price. He had exhibited it before Eastern potentates, viceroys, and maharajahs, and, of course, all the crowned heads of Europe. While I read, Tad Millgate kept at my elbow, listening to the music of a hand organ blaring through the open door, *Tramp, tramp, tramp, the boys are marching*, the same tune over and over.

As I was trying to make up my mind whether the show was worth ten cents, the professor's eye fell on Tad.

"Want a job?" he demanded, in a tone that was a royal command. "Step right inside." The professor shooed Tad into the shop and disappeared after him. I waited until he came out to give his spiel again, and parted with my dime. Inside the empty store there was no Tad, only a colored boy grinding the organ and a couple of customers looking at the long box at the end of the room. The professor came in with three customers, stood before the box and put his hand on the handsome red cloth that covered it, decorated with the professor's portrait in oils and bands of gold and silver tinsel.

"Ladies and Gentlemen!" he said with a flourish, sweeping away the cloth. Inside the glass-topped box, tiny figures were agitated in a continuous motion that, he said, stopped and started only at the sound of his voice. An old man turned a grind-stone, a woman churned, cows bobbed their heads, a dog chased a cat around a tree. We gaped and stared while he hurried through his lecture, running the words together so fast that they were almost unintelligible; but they made an impressive sound. Veiling the wonder again in the red cloth, as if he were covering a chest of jewels, he concluded, "Tell your friends to come."

Outside, I kept wondering what the professor had done with Tad. It was a week before I saw him, and when I did, he spat at the name of Professor Michael O'Grady. Tad's arm had turned the wheel that kept the little figures in perpetual motion. Cramped in the bottom of the box, he began to turn when the professor said, "Ladies and

Gentlemen!" and rested when he said, "Tell your friends to come." On Saturday when Tad and the colored boy came to get their pay, the professor had departed, owing them each a dollar and fifty cents.

I never missed a circus or a tent show, even if I had to sleep for the rest of the month on a coal car; but at the dances I was not very good, although I tried. When I was eighteen and had been firing for a couple of years, I joined the Utica Division chapter of the Brotherhood of Locomotive Firemen. Old Tom would have given me a tongue-lashing if he had known about it, but he could no longer bounce a man for joining; there were too many of us, nearly fifty percent. of his crews. The rights of labor didn't particularly agitate me, but I wanted to stick with the boys; and their overall hops were the best dances of the year. They weren't exclusive, anyone could attend who had a pair of overalls, a dollar, and a partner; but it gave me a pleasant proprietary feeling to be one of the sponsors. Even so, I was in a weak position, for I had the overalls and the dollar but no girl.

Maggie Benton, who lived next door and was the "steady" of Gander Schnell's cousin, was a good friend of mine; so I asked her what to do in such a predicament.

"I'll get you a sweetie, Joe," she promised, "one that will make their eyes stick out on toothpicks."

A few days later Maggie told me she had arranged it with Norah Dooley, who lived a couple of blocks down the street. Mother knew Mrs. Dooley. I had heard her speak of the widow, who had a hard time trying to get along by taking in washing, and of her daughter, who worked in the cotton mills; but no one prepared me for the dizzying effect of Norah.

Maggie said I must ask my partner for her company; so a few evenings later I set out to make my first call on a girl. I walked past the house several times before I mustered enough sand to pull up at the door. The widow Dooley opened it and asked me what I wanted.

"Come right in," she invited me when I asked for her daughter. "It's a fine-looking lad you are." Norah came into the parlor and asked me to sit down. As she stood in the doorway in a blue-and-white gingham dress, her gray eyes smiling at me and her coal-black hair curling about her shoulders, my heart began to pound and my voice to dry up in my throat; I wanted to sit there the rest of my life and look at her.

The night of the dance I slicked my hair with water and fussed for an hour before mother's looking-glass, trying to match up with my girl. She looked like something out of a fairy tale, with a sash around her waist and a cluster of pink rambler roses in her hair. And she knew about hops. She said I must dance the first number with her; and when we lined up in the grand march, she gave my hand an encouraging squeeze. I managed the grand right and left and swinging your partner, but when we got down to the serious business of the waltz, it was harrowing. You wouldn't think it would be so difficult to keep from stepping on those tiny feet; but wherever I put mine, they were in the wrong place. My knees ached from trying to keep them out of the way.

Finally the music died, and the struggle was over. As I

led Norah to a seat, one of the committee asked me if I would take care of the ticket booth for a little while. Norah smiled as if she was proud of me, and I was honored to be selected for such a responsible job. It was cozy in the booth, and nobody could see me kicking off my shoes to ease my trampled feet. One or two late-comers passed in their dollars and got their supper tickets, but business was light, and I had plenty of time to dream of Norah.

When I finally came out of the trance and began to notice the dancers, my heart fell with a thud to the heels of my party shoes. There was my Norah laughing and hanging on the arm of Tom Broker, fluttering her lovely eyes at him—Tom, the best dancer in town, the sport who never worked except when he needed a new suit of clothes or money to clink in his pockets. Fate had given me a shabby deal; but I had one trump left, Norah's supper ticket in my pocket. Supper-time came, and I looked everywhere—on the stairs, in the lobby, behind the band, on the stoop at the side entrance, where couples who were tired of dancing, whispered in the dark; but there was no Norah—and no Tom. Later, much later (for I sat in the booth until the last strains of *Home, Sweet Home* died away), I received the thanks of the committee and went home gloomily alone. I never saw Norah again, but I brooded about her until I heard, months afterward, that she had married Tom. Then my stricken heart recovered; but I must confess that I felt a shameful glow of pleasure, several years later, when I met Tom sweeping crossings at Genesee and Bleecker Streets.

8. The Pay-off

FOR A LONG TIME AFTER THE AFFAIR OF Norah, I put women out of my life and fell back on the more manly pleasures of hunting and fishing along the Mohawk and swimming in the canal. George Hughes, who used to make up the fire on the old Butterfly, had stayed with the Black River Line as a fireman and was expecting old John Bailey to set him up on an engine any day. He had grown up on the canal; and we spent many a summer afternoon riding the boats through the locks. George's father and mother lived on land now, in a cottage down by the yards; but his Uncle Josh and Aunt Tilly still hauled wood or whatever cargo they could get, from up-state to the docks at Rome—anything, that is, except coal. Aunt Tilly would not have the dirty stuff in the *Nelly May.*

Aunt Tilly was the cook and Uncle Josh the captain, or "old man," as canal captains were called regardless of their age. She kept little white starched curtains at the cabin window, and she fed Josh and the two steersmen on the fat of the canal stores; but she would have no cursing or rough talk at the table. When the steersmen got into fights with boats that tried to pass, or on paydays ashore, she doctored them and let them sleep off their liquor on the cargo; but she never failed to read them a sermon on the evil of their ways.

When we knew that Josh was coming down canal with a load, we sometimes caught a ride up to meet the *Nelly May*; or, failing that, walked the towpath as far as we could, listening for the distinctive note of Josh's crooked brass horn among those of the other canal boats, which echoed among the hills. Josh had his own team—a couple of heavy, well-fed horses, Prince and Bessie—and a tough little runt of a driver named Mike O'Day, who could out-shout every mule skinner on the path.

As there were no locks between Syracuse and Utica, the "long level" was a speedway, and always full of bustle and activity, as the steersmen jockeyed for position approaching Utica.

"Hurrah, Lock" they shouted; and the lock-keeper, with lungs of brass, called, "Go on, Johnny," when the boats locked through. Once I remember, George and I urged Prince and Bessie to a mild canter going through the double lock. Josh had to pay a fine of ten dollars for exceeding the four-mile speed limit. That was a staggering bill, and we had about as much chance of repaying him as we did of riding into heaven in a chariot; but we did take Aunt Tilly to a performance of "East Lynne," and I persuaded Henry to let Josh deadhead on the engine to Binghamton and back.

There was a perpetual feud between the canallers and the railroad. The canallers had been first in the field, and they considered the railroaders newcomers who were trying to push them out of business. The Lackawanna crossed the canal on a swinging bridge just east of the double lock; but the boats had right of way, and the trains couldn't get across when boats were approaching the lock. Sometimes the boats ganged up on us, and two or three trains would be stalled, waiting for them to clear. Then the shouting and cursing of railroaders and mule skinners shook the hills.

Scurrying about in the confusion were the coal pickers, the poor who gathered their fuel from the tracks. The slight tilt of the swinging bridge jolted the coal trains and shook off the top of the load, and sometimes a jimmy with faulty dumping equipment opened up, spilling coal on the track for several hundred feet. The coal pickers fell on it and carried it away in buckets, sacks, or whatever they could find.

One September morning Henry Millgate and I were stalled behind a coal train waiting for the bridge. When it finally swung around, and the train jounced across, a jimmy opened up. With a great shouting and jostling, the pickers ran to the coal. One old woman sat down by the track, spread out her dress and shovelled in the coal with both hands. When it was full, she gathered up the edge and struggled to her feet. But the strain was too much for the dress, and both it and the coal fell to the ties, leaving the woman in her naked skin. For a moment she stood there, numbed by the disaster. Then she leaned over, twisted the corners of the dress together like a sack and threw it over her shoulder.

"Hy ya, hy ya, hy ya," she shouted. An old man, picking further up the track, looked up. He answered, "Hy ya, hy ya," and climbed to his feet. Taking off his coat, he wrapped it around her and, leaving his own pile, walked with her toward a huddle of squatters' huts, doing what he could to shield her.

"Say, Joe, did you see that?" Henry asked me, not knowing whether to laugh or cry.

Before we had moved over the bridge, the old woman was back, wearing another dress. She and her gallant escort had a bucket in each hand.

We railroad men cursed the canallers and fought them. We also had some individual friends among them, but we did not play together: they lived in one world, we in another. The railroad crowd had its own dances and parties, its own ways of celebrating payday nights.

On the Lackawanna the ghost walked near the tenth of the month. At the beginning of the second week, we watched the morning passenger out of Utica, to see if her pilot carried the red flag, which meant that the pay car would be along tomorrow. After paying off the men in the shops, it started down the line, calling at every station with wages for the stationmaster, the section crews, the gandy dancers who came in on handcars, and whatever trains happened to be due.

The minute we saw the red flag, we began to figure our earnings. The married men counted that the pay for their extra runs was so much velvet, not to be included in the accounting to the wife. It was held out for a poker game, a bet on a cock fight, or a visit to John Collins' in the evening.

When we happened to meet the pay car in the home yard, there was the additional drama of wives and installment collectors gathered around the steps. Our pay car was no fancy rolling bank, with crimson stripes, lettering in gold leaf, and counters of solid mahogany, like those in the West (if you could believe the boomers); but the money that jingled inside made the same authentic clink. Ours was an old railroad coach with a cage at one end and a long table at the other, where the superintendent sat when he went along for an inspection of the road. Bill Clark, the company policeman, guarded the door, with a revolver in his belt; and in the cage, the paymaster stood behind a counter piled with stacks of silver dollars and fifty-cent pieces, quarters and nickels, which he replenished from the iron box beside him on the floor.

One by one, we came up to the window.

"Thomas Schnell, conductor, sixty-three dollars and fifty cents." The clerk called out the name and ticked it in his big ledger; the paymaster repeated it and pushed the coin through the hole in the cage, along a groove in the counter that must have been worn a quarter of an inch deep.

"Henry Millgate, engineer, sixty-one dollars and seventy-five cents." Generally Henry was in line, full of importance, ready to make a dash through the yard before the installment agents (who weren't allowed inside the car) could get up their wind. But when the odds were too heavy, Mrs. Millgate signed his name and raked in the coin. She marched out boldly, clutching it in a shabby old silk bag, and there wasn't a collector in the State of New York who dared to halt her progress.

That was the big night at John Collins'. His basement, with its rough, dark brick walls and little high windows on

a level with the street, was the gathering place of the shop-men and such of the train crews as were in off the road. Some of the more prosperous engineers and conductors patronized John O'Brien's place on Genesee Street; but there wasn't one who didn't stop in occasionally for old John's famous beer. From the keg behind the bar he drew it fresh into a brown earthenware pitcher, in which he kept a well-seasoned clay pipe. According to John, that gave the beer a special flavor. When it had settled, he poured it into a second pitcher, from which he filled the pint glasses that we called bootlegs.

On holidays and paydays, John kept a steaming bowl of Tom and Jerry on the bar beneath a shelf holding a brass pig that he had brought from Ireland years ago. It was a fat, quart-sized pig with a slot in the back and unpolished flanks, bronzed to a handsome green. John was proud of the secret keyhole under its ear. Whenever money seemed plentiful, he reminded the customers, "Have ye something to give the pig?", and when Christmas came around, he unlocked it to buy food and presents for the sick and the hurt.

The pig was John's only effort at decoration, except for a poster of a large white billy goat advertising bock beer under one of the high windows, and an old newspaper clipping offering a negro wench for sale, a "good breeder and housekeeper." The clipping was dated 1850. John kept it behind glass in a narrow gilt frame and pointed it out to every stranger.

On ordinary nights, when business was good, John sometimes favored his guests with an old Irish song and a few steps of a jig; but on payday nights the boys wanted to do their own singing. Month after month, summer or winter, sleet or shine, the payday nights were alike: shopmen settling themselves comfortably at the worn oak tables with a bootleg of beer before them and a handful of free lunch, broken crackers, and small bits of salt herring; Tom Murphy, the night watchman of the Black River Line, who was afraid of the graveyard up the track, warming up on his first bootleg to keep away the hants; one of the wrecking crew treating himself to a sandwich. John didn't serve anything but the free lunch. When a customer wanted a sandwich, he called the order to "Mother," and she brought it to the door.

John circulated among his guests with a pleasant word for everyone, stepping lightly, for all his seventy years, over the chocolate-colored sawdust, which he was always intending to renew. His white chin-whiskers were also stained, in spots, to a weathered brown; but nobody noticed, for he had an Irish friendliness that made us all feel at rights with the world.

Horace Brown, a two-hundred-pound bachelor who ran a switching engine, was there on his monthly spree. Every payday he took his money home untouched to his mother, who gave him back a dollar and advised him not to spend it all at once. But he was a reckless man and said he was for a good time once a month, whatever it cost.

After his second bootleg, Horace was so pleased with himself that he burst into a song—the only one he knew, the *Sword of Bunker Hill*; and after the third or fourth drink, happy tears ran down his cheeks. Sometimes Herman Crouse, the one-legged crossing watchman, with whiskers landscaped like those of the Emperor Francis Joseph, accompanied Horace on an accordion, beating time with his wooden leg. Everyone was happy, singing or weeping after his fashion, banishing for a few hours the anxieties, disappointments, and failures of the month.

Cigar smoke, a bootleg with the foam on it sitting before you, a friend boasting about the run he made last week, another telling a new one on the Old Man, you matching him with the tale about the day Henry lost his hind end somewhere beyond Oxford and never missed it until he looked for Gander in the lunchroom at Norwich (and how Gander nearly paralyzed his Adam's apple with rage, when he had to walk all the way in)—all these made John Collins' a comfortable, friendly place. And it was a decent place: no cursing or fighting or rowdy talk; John wouldn't stand for it. Neither would we, because in a very special sense the place belonged to us. It was our club. Outside we might brawl as much as we liked, and roar like fighting bulls; but while we drank John's beer and ate his herrings, we were such good friends that we would do anything in the world for each other.

9. The Triumph of Sitting Bull

AT LAST THE OLD MAN PUT ME ON THE schedule, firing the local freight that ran to Binghamton and back, twelve hours each day. It stopped at every station, sometimes on the blind sidings, and holed up like a rabbit to keep out of the way of the fast trains; but it *was* on the schedule—a regular train.

Dad Burr, the pilot, a good-natured, plump old dandy with a magnificent white beard, had descended from the through freights and passengers when the strain of the fast runs began to wear him down; and he had settled into the comfortable tempo of this drag for the rest of his life. A bachelor and a lady-killer, he went to the Saturday night dances, beaued the girls, and lived at ease in the best room of the old railroad boardinghouse in Utica (twenty-five cents for a meal—any meal—and twenty-five cents for a bed). To him the run was not work but a chance to visit with the station agents, a social round on which from one stop to the next he carried news of everything that happened up and down the line.

The conductor, Hank Smith ("Sitting Bull," Dad called him), was no speedier than Dad. Both of them were too lazy to lift an oilcan or feel for a hotbox; but each blamed the other for delays, and the feud was one of the liveliest running battles of the division. The boys warned me that I would have to do most of the work; but the lazier Dad was, the better I liked it—I would have a chance to run the engine.

Now that I was to spend every other night in Binghamton and had been promoted from "extra" to a full-time job on a regular run, I decided to stop sleeping on coal cars and the floor of the caboose and treat myself to a bed in the Grove Hotel. On the first night in, I went across the tracks to the faded, square, shabby old building in front of which railroad men were already gathering, filling the row of slat-backed chairs that stood side by side, nailed to a long plank at regular intervals, their backs against the wall.

Pushing through the battered oak door with its panel of sanded glass, I entered the lobby. This was the first time I had seen the interior of a hotel, so I looked curiously about the big room with its dado of varnished yellow oak, topped by a band of faded paper. A row of split-bottomed chairs near the window, a large china spittoon filled with sand and cigar-butts, and a chandelier dangling two fly-specked oil lamps, were the only furnishings, except for a gaudy advertising calendar above the counter which served as a desk. Behind the desk Denny, a short, querulous Irishman, was looking at me with an unhappy air.

Hoping he would not know how green I was, I swung my lunch pail carelessly as I went over and ordered a room.

"Where do you work?" Denny asked, giving me a hostile eye. Not satisfied by my answer that I was a fireman on the railroad, he demanded to know where I came from, and when I told him Utica, he glared at me and danced a sort of turkey strut behind the counter.

"Utica," he shouted, "Utica! I wouldn't trust a Utica man, no more than I'd trust my life to the devil."

The men on the front porch stuck their heads through the windows to see the fun. Glancing over my shoulder, hoping that Dad and Sitting Bull weren't witnesses to this humiliation, I saw Gander Schnell ambling through the door. He made an accurate shot at the spittoon and leaned across the desk.

"Pipe down, Denny," he said. "It ain't no crime to be from Utica. The kid's all right, he has fired for me. You ain't got anybody in the Utica room. Go ahead and give it to him." The show was over. Gander gave me a friendly pat and went back onto the porch, and the heads dropped out of the windows. Grumbling, Denny took a big iron key from the board, led me down an unlighted corridor to number twenty-three and opened the door to a bare room containing a couple of kitchen chairs, a washstand and two nicked iron beds. One of the beds had fancy curlicues and a single, dented brass knob stuck on at a cockeyed angle. The others, I guessed, had been kicked off by the Utica men.

"I may have to put someone in the other bed," Denny told me. "You see, this room has an outside door so you railroad men can leave when you are called in the middle of the night, without waking me. That's the reason you have to pay in advance." Denny said he would send up some hot water. He was almost friendly when he brought me a couple of gray towels and looked at the lamp to see that it had been filled.

After I washed up, I ate one of mother's good beef sandwiches and a piece of cake and walked down Henry Street to loaf on a corner and watch the girls. This was the local custom. The young bucks braced up the lamp posts, waiting for the girls coming home from the cigar factories.

"Hello, sister. Got any scrap?" they asked, and the girls dug into their deep, two-foot pockets for the tobacco, which they had saved for their favorite beaus. In those days the girls could carry home all of the scrap they wanted, but later the companies sold it in five-cent packages. One big Irish girl, with red hair and the greenest eyes I ever saw, had smiled at me on other evenings and taught me how to crumble the scrap and roll it into cigarettes. We spent several hours taking the long route to her home, which was only a couple of blocks away.

When I came back to the Utica room, the other bed was empty. That was luck. I settled in for a good night's sleep, but had scarcely buried my ear in the pillow when there was a scratching on the outer door.

"Joe, Joe," came a squeaky whisper through the key-hole. "It's me, Andy." Andy was the hind brakeman on Dad's freight.

"Thanks, pal," he said when I opened the door, and before I locked it, he had stripped off his overalls and climbed into the other bed. I bumped over a chair in the dark, found my own bed and turned my face to the wall, hoping Andy wouldn't snore; but I had not gone to sleep when there was a rat-tat-tat of knuckles on the same door.

"Hold it, kid," called Andy. He jumped out of bed and whispered through the keyhole. "It's Bert Clark, a shack on Number 6," he told me, and opened up. Bert got into

bed with Andy and all was quiet, but not for long. Again a rattle of the door. This time Bert got up. It was like a game—last man in, first man out. Before one o'clock we were seven—the two shacks and a fireman in Andy's bed, and a couple of shacks from the coal trains in mine. With the whispering and bumping in the dark, we roused Denny.

"Sh-h, there's the old man," groaned the brakie next to me, as we heard bare feet flapping along the corridor. Denny pounded on the door.

"How many have you in your room, Bromley?"

"Nobody but me," I answered.

"Open up while I look."

"Tell him you can't find the key," whispered Andy.

"Can't find the key," I shouted.

"All right," called Denny, "I'll go down and get mine."

There was a scramble in the dark, overturned chairs, thumping of boots, screeching of the outer door. When Denny came back with his key and a round-handled glass lamp, which threw a yellow light over the sawed-off bean-poles holding up his nightshirt, my bed was empty of all except me, and Andy was the only man left in the other.

"I didn't want to get you up late, Denny, old man," Andy said, grinning at the sputtering Irishman. "Throw me my jeans and I'll give you the two bits."

Denny took his money and slammed the door.

"Poor Denny." Andy chuckled before he turned over to pound his ear, "he gets it going and coming. He goes through this performance almost every night."

Denny must have given better quarters to Dad and Hank and Gander, the aristocracy of the road, for none but the shacks and firemen turned up in the Utica room. We didn't mind the interrupted sleep, for we were young and liked the game. Hauling the local freight was a vacation for me after the coal; in good weather it was more of an art than a heavy-muscle job. We spent most of the day on sidetracks with Andy on top of one of the middle cars, waving Dad forward, slowing him, easing a loaded car to a stop at the freight platform. And Dad had the lightest hand on the throttle that I had ever seen—no backing and filling. He and Andy worked like one brain, and he gentled the engine with such delicate precision that he spotted the car plump in front of the freight house doors on the first try.

Dad had an understanding with Andy, who gave him the tip-off when there was a heavy consignment that would take some time to unload. With a flourish that Sitting Bull couldn't miss, he put on his jacket and went over to the station to visit. While Dad loafed, Hank worked; he had to break the seal on the boxcar doors, roll them back, give a set of waybills to the agent and check his own bill against the agent's as the shacks rolled out the freight.

"Five bales of hay for Bailey's." The agent ticked it off.

"Three black diamond wood stoves for Christie's Hardware, two kegs of nails, and six rolls of chicken wire.

"Six boxes of crackers, three of cheese, and five boxes of canned goods for General Mercantile.

"One parlor sofa for Mrs. Gannon. . . . How come she's getting furniture? The old man loosening up?"

The agent made a thumb hole in the heavy paper wrappings and looked at the upholstery. "Light blue. Right pretty. Yeah, Gannon's having to spend a dime. His Lucy's getting married to the superintendent of the sawmill. Careful there, boys, don't knock it against the door. Hank, did you come across that box of shoes for Harris' store? He's raising hell."

"Yeah," Hank would answer. "It got stuck in the wrong car and was thrown off at Paris. Tell him to keep his shirt on, we'll bring it along tomorrow."

When the unloading was finished, and Hank had smoked

a pipe with the agent, he signalled me to toot the whistle, and Dad made a leisurely exit from the station.

After a few trips I knew all about the feud between Dad and Hank—all, that is, but its unbelievable conclusion. The agent at Oxford was an old-timer, a brass-pounder who had broken down his wrists in lonely little stations from Maine to the Pacific before he settled on a pocket-sized farm just outside of Oxford. The office didn't stay open at night, so at five o'clock he locked up and went home to feed the chickens and milk his one Holstein cow. The buxom daughter who kept house for him insisted on bringing Pop a hot dinner every day, and generally managed to be there when we came through—late on our down trip and early on the return. She had an easy way with her and played Dad against Hank with cheerful impartiality.

Dad was free with his money. Sometimes he took her to Norwich with us on the engine and set her up to a restaurant meal served by Santa Claus, with bakery creampuffs and all the fixings. Hank was a married man and labored under a disadvantage; but he and Andy had the caboose fixed up with cushions on the bunk-bench and a scrap of oilcloth in front of the stove. Andy cooked superior fried chicken, when he was lucky enough to steal a bird from the farmers' chicken coops after dark; and Hank stretched his pocketbook to bring along oranges and an occasional can of sardines—store things that would be a treat to a woman on a farm. When Ellie was in the caboose dining with Hank and Andy, Dad swore that Hank carried a keg of nails to put on and off at Oxford, just to pretend he had a waybill. He wouldn't be caught leaning out the window, but he couldn't escape the inviting smell of the chicken.

"Come on, Joe," he said to me, "bank your fire. Let's go down to the river and see if we can get a fish. It will be another hour before Sitting Bull gets through stuffing food into Pretty-face. Did you ever notice how Hank leans against the car door when he's checking the manifest, and absent-mindedly scratches his back against the side? Just like a buffalo. I used to see them on the priaries. When the Union Pacific ran a telegraph line through, the buffaloes used the poles for back-scratchers, pushed them over faster than the Supe could put them up. It was always a good alibi for lost time to say that we had to stop and throw the poles off the track. Then the Supe bought all the shoe-makers' awls between Chicago and Omaha and nailed them on the poles to keep the critters off; but the buffaloes liked the awls even better than the bare poles. That's the stuff! We could tack an awl on the door for old Sitting Bull." Pleased with his idea, Dad forgot his ill-humor and got out his fishing line. His overload of fat around the waist shook like jelly when I handed him down the bank.

Sitting Bull was not so amiable when Dad kept him wait-ing at Norwich, while he and Ellie supped their coffee.

"You go tell old Sheep-face that if he doesn't get this train moving, I'll report him to the superintendent," he sputtered to me. Of course I never did, and Hank hadn't intended that I should.

The summer wore on, and it was autumn. Andy was promoted to extra conductor and married the girl who lived on the farm across the lake at Pooleville. All summer he had watched her white dishcloth hanging on the line, a signal that she was expecting him on Sunday, and worried about the farmer who helped her father with the chores.

The fall rains came, and the new brakeman was not so quick with his signals as he teetered on the roofs, dripping like a half-drowned pigeon. Dad watched him out the window and cursed as he pushed the screaming wheels back and forth on the wet rails, trying to spot the cars.

But neither rain nor hail nor sleet dampened Ellie's devotion to her Pop. Almost every day she was at the Oxford station, joshing with Dad and Hank. She hemstitched a red-and-white checked tablecloth for the hinged shelf-table in the caboose, which Hank let down to write his orders; and for Dad she was knitting a yellow muffler, which she carried about in a paper bag with the needles sticking out.

One day Dad told me that he had promised to take her to Binghamton shopping, adding hastily that she had a cousin in town with whom she would spend the night. Ellie was at the station, almost bursting out of a tight basque with mutton-leg sleeves that took up half of the cab, and a bonnet tall enough to hit the roof. I gave her my seat and went into the tender with the front shack, but it was going to be a ticklish job getting a lump of coal past that balloon of creaking silk. At Coventry and Brisben I got out and oiled around for Dad, thinking it more polite to leave him and Ellie alone. Hank was in a fierce temper and slung off the manifest as if he were handling hot coals.

While we were unloading at Brisben, the sun disappeared, the wind began to whip up the river and rain fell in gusts, spitting into our faces. By the time we had reached the Grecian Bend, it was pitch-black outside. Dad slowed down to two or three miles an hour. The shack lighted the headlight, but it was swallowed up in the rain; so he rode the pilot. He was the farthest thing we could see, hunched in a wet bundle with his head thrust forward.

Thunder cracked above the booming of the wheels and lightning burned jagged holes in the dark, first on one side, then the other. Ellie screamed and clung to Dad, gripping him in a vise—babbling that he would have to protect her, she would never leave him. Smothered in her sleeves, he looked at me grimly. We weren't using much steam, so I kept my eye on the works. Ellie had Dad backed away from the window into the corner, and every time the lightning flashed, she shrieked and covered his beard with teary kisses. Somehow I got the impression that she was making the most of the storm. Wedged in front of them, I peered through the water slithering down the front window and caught the brakie's signal that the siding at Greene was clear.

"Take Ellie into the station," I suggested to Dad. "I'll unload and keep up steam."

I helped them down from the engine and watched them stumble along the ties to the station door. We didn't have much of a load for Greene, so it didn't take long to get rid of the freight, even though the shacks had to work by lantern light. The rain made such a thick curtain that they looked like ghosts moving about in misty haloes, though no farther than a half-dozen cars away. Presently Hank gave me the highball with the lantern, and I tooted for

Dad. He came out and made a run for the engine. Easing out the throttle, he picked up the slack, and we crawled out onto the main track with a clearance for Binghamton. Then he slumped on his cushion and squeezed the water out of his beard.

"She's going to stay here all night with the agent's wife," he said, keeping his eyes fixed on the oilcans in the corner.

"Oh, hell, Joe," he exploded. "I'm in a fix. That gal's got her hooks in me, and I never want to lay eyes on Pretty-face again. She thinks we're going to pick her up in the morning, but I'm going to wire Sam to tell her we had a breakdown and to put her on another train. Be a good kid, Joe, when we get in, and keep old Sitting Bull off of me. He'll be eating his tonsils out to know what happened, and I ain't going to give him the satisfaction of finding out."

The next morning when we pulled out, the sunshine was so bright it made your blood dance. Dad scorched the rails, slinging the manifest around as if we were dragging a string of empty matchboxes, until he came to Greene. As we slid onto the loading track, he turned the throttle over to me and scrooched down in the tender. When Hank saw my face hanging out of the window, he came back to see what was wrong.

"What happened to old Sheep-face? Did he have a stroke?"

"No, no," I said nervously, "he just got off to get a drink."

When we pulled out, Dad took over until we came within sight of the red barn on the Harris farm at the edge of Oxford. Then he took another dive into the tender. After I spotted the first car and made sure that Ellie wasn't anywhere around, I took Dad's oilcan and jumped down to look over the engine. Coming along the ties on the off side was Sitting Bull, looking at his wheels.

"Joe," he called to me softly, "tell old Sheep-face we ain't lingering."

I climbed in, told Dad that all was clear, and repeated Hank's message. Dad came out of the coal, dusted himself off, smoothed his beard and settled on his cushion with a grunt of relief.

"So old Sitting Bull got an earful from Sam at Greene. I thought he would rib me about it, but I guess he's as frightened as I am, and thinks she'll concentrate on him."

From that day Dad and Sitting Bull were closer than brothers. Every time we took the siding at Oxford, they were inseparable—Dad back at the loading car, helping Sitting Bull, giving a hand with the freight. They joshed Ellie as if nothing had happened, but they took care that neither one was left with her alone; and there were no more trips to Norwich or chicken dinners in the caboose. After a while she brought her father's dinner at noon and wasn't around when we came through. She never hem-stitched the napkins to match Hank's tablecloth, and the yellow muffler I saw around the neck of a fireman on the local passenger.

One evening I told mother about Dad and Sitting Bull,

marveling that they should have become such friends. Mother wrinkled up her nose. You could tell she felt sorry for Ellie, the way her eyes snapped.

"Isn't it wonderful," she said, "the way men hang together?"

10. The Old Man Eats Dirt

I LOST THE ALLIGATOR WRENCH WHEN WE were shifting around Waterville last night," Dad told me. "Let's lift one off the Old Man."

Getting supplies from Tom Thatcher was harder than pulling a lung with your teeth; he expected a fellow to haul a drag to Binghamton and back on a quart of oil, and he even begrudged us an extra handful of waste. But there were ways of getting around him, and every man on his call board tried to think of a new one.

"I'll go to the office and ask for a new headlight chimney, and you go to Johnny to fill up your oilcan. While he's drawing it, you sneak into the storeroom and grab the wrench. The Old Man will be so busy swearing at me that he won't look out the window."

I waited until Dad had time to get Old Tom started; then while Johnny was drawing the oil on the other side of the tank, I got a wrench and stuck it in my jeans. Drifting around to the front of the yard office, I leaned against the wall to enjoy the Old Man's performance. The window and door were wide open to catch whatever breeze was stirring on this hot September afternoon.

Green sand flies buzzed in and out, and, above their droning, Tom was blasting the air with oaths fierce and magnificent.

Presently Dad came out and winked at me as he mopped his beaded head. I nodded, and we started along to the roundhouse.

"Jumping Jehoshaphat, look who's here." He stopped dead and shoved his thumb toward the yard gate, through which we saw the Sheriff, the Mayor, the State Senator, and a couple of aldermen stepping gingerly across the tracks. Fanning themselves with their hats, the delegation made for Old Tom's office, with Dad and me at a respectful distance. We risked a peep through the window and saw them line up before the judgment bar, with the Senator in the middle. Rogers, the clerk, was beckoning to the Old Man. We ducked our heads and listened. The Senator, oozing cordiality, said that he and these gentlemen, all candidates in the coming local election, had called to ask the Master Mechanic's permission to address the men at the noon hour. He was sure the road would want its employees to understand the issues involved in the campaign.

No, snorted the Old Man, the Lackawanna did *not* want its employees mixed up with vile politicians, and neither did he. The quicker these gentlemen removed themselves from the company's property, the better it would suit him. This curt statement Old Tom adorned with a collection of his fanciest oaths.

Dad and I left even quicker than the vile politicians. All the way over the hump and through the swamp we talked about Tom's unreasonableness in depriving us of a celebration; and when we stopped for water at the Grecian Bend, we consulted Sitting Bull and the shacks. They had no immediate plan to offer, but when we got back to Utica and dropped our boxcars in the yard, we learned by the stovepipe route that the matter had already been taken care of. Rogers had leaked to several of the old-timers in the shops, who had written a letter to the Mayor regretting the discourteous treatment that the committee had received from the Master Mechanic and inviting the candidates to address the men on Saturday afternoon, when the work week closed at three o'clock. The field known as the Goose Pasture back of the enginehouse was owned jointly by the Lackawanna and the New York, Ontario & Western railroads and would make an admirable place for the meeting. Refreshments would be in order, if the committee cared to bring them. We saw the document before it was mailed—a handsome example of Rogers' flowing Spencerian penmanship.

The Mayor sent word that the refreshments and the candidates would be on hand the following Saturday at the appointed time. Most of us managed to be there; because Mr. Sloan, the President, was a righteous man and had decreed that no trains on the Lackawanna should run on Sunday. If a train was unable to make its terminal by midnight Saturday night, it finished the run Sunday morning; but not a wheel rolled out of the yards on the Sabbath.

Saturday was a perfect day for a rally. The sun gilded the dust on the flat wheels, old running gear, broken pistons, and rusty piles of other abandoned equipment, which made convenient lounging-places for the boys. They gathered promptly and watched the brewery wagon drive up behind its heavy, matched gray Percherons. Some of them gave a hand and rolled barrels of beer to a plank table set up on a couple of horses. On one end of the planks were stacked loaves of bread, and along its length were piles of Bologna sausages and Limburger cheese, which an alderman was carving in generous hunks. The Senator arrived in a carriage and began to shake hands; the Mayor passed out cigars. In front of the table the three members of the brass band (a drum and two horns) stuck handkerchiefs under their hot red collars.

On an old flatcar slightly tilted because of a flattened wheel, the Mayor made a welcoming address. Nobody listened. We all rolled the cigars patiently in our mouths, with our eyes on the table, behind which one of the aldermen was using his hat as a fly brush. Everyone knew and observed the etiquette of the rally: first the speeches, then the rush to the tables and the fun.

Finally the Mayor worked himself up to a fervid, perspiring climax. Everybody shouted, the Senator uncorked a barrel and the boys made for the tables. Nick Kuhn grinned at me as he stuffed his pockets full of cigars, and Gander Schnell began to eat a slice of Limburger, his Adam's apple working up and down with the steady rhythm of a piston.

At the height of the fun a hush began to creep over the crowd. One man whispered to another, until the only sound was the tipsy singing of a brakeman on an upturned boxcar, shouting *Rock of Ages* between long gulps of beer. His back was toward the yard, and he did not see the Old Man coming across the field. Everybody waited, rooted in his place, as Old Tom strode between the junk piles, bareheaded, his whiskers fanning out in his own wind and his arms flailing the air.

"Begone!" he shouted, as soon as he came within hailing distance. "Begone, you vile varmints. Get out of here!"

The boys crowded back and left the Mayor standing alone in the Old Man's path. Someone overturned the table, hunks of Limburger rolled under the junk, and from an unplugged beer barrel a stream of suds made rivulets through the dusty grass.

Before the Mayor, Old Tom put on the brakes, hissing through his whiskers, his good eye shooting sparks of wrath. Unctuously the Mayor greeted him, sticking out the hand of welcome. Through the kindness of the New York, Ontario & Western Railway they were using the field for the afternoon, he said. Wouldn't Mr. Thatcher join in the festivities? Perhaps he would say a few words to the men.

"God damn ye," the Old Man shouted, "I *will* have a few words to say. Get out of here in five minutes, or I'll send for the police!" The Mayor smiled, the Senator smiled and came forward as if to shake Tom's hand, an alderman smiled and slapped him playfully on the shoulder.

Old Tom drew back, confused, routed, but still spouting fire. His good eye, darting around, fell upon Scoopie, an old-timer who did odd jobs around the shop. Sitting high on a pile of driving-wheels, Scoopie was grinning with delight, so overjoyed that he was tipping his glass of beer, dribbling it down his front. The Old Man fixed him with his good eye.

"Go to the office and get your time," he shouted.

"Go to hell," Scoopie shouted back, downing the beer.

The men broke into a wild cheer, the drummer thumped and the horns blared out *Auld Lang Syne* as Old Tom retreated across the field, strutting, his head in the air and his shoulders rearing back. At the enginehouse he turned and shook his fist.

The Senator climbed on the flatcar and orated, the aldermen orated, the band blared and the men downed their beer and Limburger. When we had eaten the last of the Bologna and cleaned out the cigar boxes, we went home with our arms around each other, shouting and singing. Not one of us could remember a word of the speeches; all were thinking about the Old Man.

Monday morning we were at work again, even Scoopie; but we eased into the enginehouse without lingering around the yard office. The Old Man was mum, and the only reminder of his defeat was a notice on the bulletin board that read:

"All employees found drinking intoxicating liquors on or near the property of the company will be dismissed from the service.

Signed, Thomas Thatcher"

But Old Tom hadn't lost his grip. His curses split the air from the shop to the roundhouse, to the office, and we all settled back into the old routine. Only one of the men stuck up for the "Master Maniac": Soapy Freeman, an engineer who had come over from the main line when Henry Millgate broke his shoulder trying to pull a cook-stove off the tender, as he was taking it home to Schuyler Street.

"You don't get Tom right," Soapy told us one day, when he was assigned to take us out in place of Dad, who was down with the grippe. "Tom's really got a kind heart and is as considerate and gentle as a lamb, if you go at him the right way. You fellows let him get your goat. You ought to be easy and jolly with him. We went to school together and were just like brothers. It ain't hard to get along with him."

Sitting Bull, who had come up to the cab window with Soapy's orders, snorted and went back to the "crummy" (caboose), waggling his black mustache. He must have spread the news; for every time we pulled into a station to unload, the shacks came front and asked Soapy what was the best way to get along with the Old Man.

Soapy was a good runner. He could pick up slack without knocking out the hind brakeman's teeth and scattering the brains' orders over the right of way; but on the return trip he was logy. It was a drowsy afternoon, too warm for September, with not a breath of air to carry away the fumes of the steam, mixed with the smell of oil and the acrid odor of the coal. When we ran into the long stretch through the swamp, the fire didn't need much watching, it was burning well, and old 18 was bucking along with the throttle wide open, making a great clatter. Soapy lolled back on his cushion, with his eyes half closed and his hands in his lap. I was leaning over with my back to the window, drowsily chiselling a lump of coal for the rat-hole, when the front shack let out a squawk that tumbled Soapy off his seat. He had been sound asleep with his mouth hanging open.

Snapping up first, I looked out the front window, grabbed the lever, threw it in the big hole, yelled to Soapy and jumped for the ties, just as the pilot nosed up the caboose of a train in front. As I hit the granite, the engineer from the wrecked caboose leaped for the rails, clutching a handful of waybills; but the brakeman still perched in the cupola. We could see his legs dangling above the hole in what was left of the back wall.

By that time Sitting Bull and the hind shack were on the ties, running toward the engine. Soapy had picked himself up and was rubbing his eyes.

"Were you blind?" shouted the conductor of the stalled freight. "You overran our flag."

"Just taking his afternoon nap." Sitting Bull's voice was acid with contempt. "If it hadn't been for this kid, who spotted you in the cupola, we'd have piled you up like a heap of jackstraws. What you stopping for?"

The conductor of the freight showed us a hanging brake beam. Luckily no brakeman was underneath when we hit. One of them was already crawling under with a wrench, and it didn't look like more than a fifteen-minute job. Our hind brakeman, the boy who had been in the cupola, took the red flag out of our caboose and went back to relieve the other shack and flag the coal train, which was already showing smoke behind us. We looked at the damage: a smashed headlight and a few gouges in the paint, made by the splintered wood.

Scotty Barnes, running the coal behind us, slid up to within a few yards of our crummy and came over with his shack to see what was going on. Already the highball freight was also pushing up the valley; we could see the thick end of her plume of smoke as she left Sangerfield.

For twenty minutes we stood along the track, picking cinders out of our arms, cleaning the splintered back wall of the freight's caboose from the track and listening to the hoots of the engineer on the fast freight stalled behind the coal. Finally the battered freight limped into the siding at Brookfield. We followed, and Scotty's drag had to hole up at Waterville, keeping the fast freight held down to fifteen miles an hour. The eagle-eye of the freight waved derisively at Sitting Bull as he crawled by.

The lightning-slinger came out onto the platform of the Brookfield station with a green shade over his eyes and waved an order at Sitting Bull.

"The Supe is burning out the wires. You boys sure did ball up the line. You've got the local passenger stalled at Paris, and you've stabbed the freight for half an hour—not to mention the coal trains lined up this side of Norwich. I can't put you through for a couple of hours."

Soapy went in to moan with the brass-pounder. Sitting Bull and the conductor of the freight went fishing in the Chenango and came back with a mess of little fish not much bigger than minnows, which they fried in our caboose and passed around. I played seven-up with the boy who had been in the cupola. It was his first week on the road, and he was white and jumpy. He couldn't even eat a piece of mother's apple pie.

At about dusk Soapy whistled us in and took over. He had managed to tie on a makeshift headlight with a reflector made from part of an old tin coal scuttle that the station agent dug up. We had to hole in at Paris for another couple of hours, but we gained a little time on the downgrade. Sitting Bull said we might as well get in before the Old Man burst a blood vessel.

"Leave Tom to me," said Soapy jauntily, spitting steam from his cylinder cocks. "He's a good fellow at heart. You just don't understand him."

"Go to it." Sitting Bull grinned at me and shrugged.

Scratching the face of an engine and taking the back wall out of a caboose are serious enough in any railroad man's language; but what the Old Man would say about it, we didn't try to guess. If a fireman twisted his back heaving coal or a brakeman smashed a finger or a leg, it was bad luck; Tom was sorry and did what he could, although he generally thought it was the man's own fault. But when anything happened to his equipment, he was a snarling tiger.

It was almost midnight when we slid across the drawbridge and into the yards. The Old Man was waiting for us—we could see the dark bulk of him standing in the light of the open yard office door. He was charging across the yard before we had dropped off the cars and pulled up to the roundhouse. Sitting Bull got very busy with his orders, and the three shacks kept behind him with their ears stretched; but Soapy ran the engine onto the turntable and jumped out of the cab before she had stopped rolling.

"Hello, Tom," he called. "We had a little trouble down the line—ran into a freight. She was short-flagged, but, thank God, we only punched a hole in the caboose."

"Punched a hole in the caboose! You Goddamned snivelling idiot! You needn't think you can come over from the main line and smash up my equipment. You yellow-livered son of a mule skinner. You never were any good. Even when you went to school, your father had to drag you out of every bawdy-house on Water Street. God blast you for smashing up my engine! Get your time. Scat, before I get my hands on you!" Old Tom's last string of oaths sputtered hoarsely in his beard, and the glass eye shone like a live coal in the path of the headlight.

As Soapy backed into the enginehouse, Sitting Bull pinched my arm. We grinned at each other sheepishly, proud as hell of the Old Man.

11. Promotion

THE WINTERS AND SUMMERS GLIDED BY like haystacks moving across the cab window—although each one of them had seemed an eternity when it stretched before me, inviting as the rails running endlessly before the pilot. I knew every sag and curve in the road from Binghamton to Utica, could hit the firebox door from the farthest corner of the tender and could spot a car at a freight stop almost as neatly as Dad. The Old Man had moved me from the local to the highball freight, and in the summer of '87 had put me on the regular passenger run to Richfield Springs. The season was well along when the operator at Richfield Junction came out to the engine one afternoon with a message for me, an order to report to Mr. Thatcher on arrival.

"Don't look so serious, Joe," the operator said, taking off his eye shade and scratching his ear. "The Old Man ain't going to bounce you. I hear he's gong to promote some engineers."

I thanked him and hoped he was right, but as I sat idle while the eagle-eye cut off the steam and coasted down the hill, I kept wondering what I might have done.

It was late afternoon when we got in. I went over to the yard office and looked through the door. Rogers, who was hanging a ribbon of fly paper to the reflector of the light over his desk, smiled at me encouragingly; so I walked in, trying to look self-possessed, and stood with my cap draped over the judgment bar. Old Tom came out from behind his high, roll-topped desk and glared at me. At least, I thought he was glaring, as the sun through the western window reflected on his kindlier eye.

"Well," he spluttered through his front teeth, "you're here at last. You're five minutes late, but I suppose you've got an alibi. I've hired the last Goddamned boomer that's ever going to work on this road, and I'm going to promote my own boys, even if they ain't dry behind the ears."

Rogers grinned at me behind the Old Man's back. It was common knowledge that the Master Mechanic had been in a temper for a week—ever since a couple of boomer engineers had staged a cornfield meet in the Norwich yards, killing a foreman and ruining one of Tom's best freight engines.

"Do you think you know enough to run an engine and keep her bearings from cutting?"

"Yes, sir," I answered.

"Don't be too damned sure. You always know too much." The Old Man stamped up and down with his hands behind his back, thinking of his wrongs. When I was easing myself back onto my heels, sure that he had forgotten me, he turned and snapped, "Do you know your rights over the road?"

Meekly I repeated the rules about right, class, and direction, telling him that right is conferred by train order, class and direction by the timetable.

"Well," he said, "I'll send you out. It's robbing the cradle, but I'll take a chance. It's up to you. If anything happens, don't come to me. Get out and streak for home before I kick you out."

The Old Man spat neatly into the brass cuspidor and went back to his desk. The examination was at an end. Rushing out into the yard, I wanted to shout and pummel someone, to run to John Collins' and set up the whole town to a glass of beer. I was twenty and an engineer, the youngest on the road.

The first man I met was my cousin, Jerry, a fireman on the coal. He had an order in his hand and was streaking anxiously toward the yard office.

"Oh, boy," he shouted, looking at my face. "You got promoted. What kind of examination did the Old Man give you?" I told him it was nothing to be afraid of, but warned him not to be too cocksure. He nodded and gripped my hand. When Old Tom asked him if he knew enough to oil the engine and keep his bearings from cutting, he answered hesitantly, "I think so."

"Think!" roared the Old Man. "Damn you, you're always thinking. Go back to do your thinking while you're firing coal." Jerry didn't get promoted for two months, and he had it in for me.

The first job Old Tom gave me was loading wheels. He called me into the office and turned me over to the Wrecking Master, Lindquist, a mighty, six-foot Swede with a face full of yellow whiskers.

PROMOTION

"If you break Lindquist's chain," Tom threatened, "you'll get laid off for the rest of the day, and set back ten Brownies." The big Swede scowled at me for emphasis.

We went into the yard and I climbed into the right-hand side of the engine attached to his outfit—a derrick on a flatcar, with which he cleared the track after accidents and moved heavy material to the shops, the storage sheds, or the eventual junk pile. The engine gave me confidence, for she was my first love on the Lackawanna. Now that she had grown too light for the road, she had been demoted to the yard; but she was a beauty, one of the finest engines of her day. Her name was the *Lewis Lawrence* and she was Number 1, neat and handsomely stripped with brass, her works put together with the delicate precision of a watch. I had fired her and remembered her bell, which took a particularly high polish. When she was built in Schenectady, Mr. Lawrence, the stockholder for whom she was named, put twenty-eight silver dollars in the brass from which the bell was cast; and it was the silver, according to the men in the shop, that gave her a tone higher and truer than any other.

A year or so later I came upon Number 1 being towed across the yard, her bell and trimmings stripped and dumped into a boxcar tied to her tender. I wanted that silver bell and tried to get it from the car before it was dragged to Scranton and the junk pile, but I had no luck.

On this morning when the Old Man sent me to load flat wheels that were being taken into the shop for scrap, she purred under my hand like a beautiful cat. The chain, about which Old Tom had warned me, hoisted two wheels at a time, lifted them with the pulley on the derrick and dumped them into a flatcar that was coupled to the engine. When the engine moved forward, she moved the derrick and lifted the wheels. My job was to creep ahead a few feet at a time, and if I didn't stop on a pinhead, I was sure to break the chain. After a few tries I saw that Number 1 was willing but slow in answering to the brake, and asked Lindquist to give me the stop signal a fraction of a second earlier. The Swede said he would, but he was very little help—he was too busy pushing around his handful of workmen, trying to ape the Old Man.

During the morning, while the men rolled the cumbersome wheels to the derrick, Lindquist made frequent disappearances. From my perch in the cab, I watched him crawl through a hole in the board fence and hightail it in the direction of the Widow Wosner's saloon across the road. Each time when he came back, his signals were a little less accurate. The chain was going to break—I knew it. The harder I tried, the less I could do to avoid it; and the more bitter grew my sense of injury, thinking that I was going to get my first black mark in four years on my first day behind the throttle, because this big ox of a Swede was tippling on the job.

Just before noon the chain snapped, and the yard hands leaped out of the way as the wheels fell back on the ties with an ear-splitting clatter. Lindquist bore down upon the cab, swearing through his bush of whiskers.

"Well," he shouted, "you know what the Old Man said. You might as well scat. I have to go and tell him now."

I stood up in the cab, clutching a wrench, boiling with indignation but taking care to keep out of the reach of the Swede.

"Wait a minute," I shouted back, trying to keep my voice steady. "I'm going with you to the office. Mr. Thatcher will be interested to know about your trips to the Widow Wosner's. You know very well you were slow with the signals."

Lindquist glared at me, at the fireman and the men, who kept their heads turned away to hide their quirking lips.

"A sucker, eh?" he roared, flexing his arms.

"No, it's just a matter of duty. You report the broken chain, I tell how it happened."

"Well, what the hell can I do?" the Swede muttered in his beard.

"You might go to the blacksmith," I suggested, trying to keep the antagonism out of my voice, although I was still boiling inside. "Bill's a good sport. He'll weld the chain before the Old Man gets back from lunch, if you'll give him a quarter or promise him a glass of beer."

Lindquist scowled, but he dragged the chain out of the pulley, threw it over his shoulder and clumped away in the direction of the blacksmith's shop. The yard men, delighted at the lay-off, sat around on the wheels for a long lunch hour, trading stories over their coffee and hunks of bread and cheese. They were already making a saga out of the incident and treated me like a new Paul Bunyan.

Lindquist came back at one o'clock with the mended chain, and we all fell to work in good humor. When the

Old Man came around in the afternoon to see how the job was getting on, he was surprised and—perhaps I imagined it—a shade disappointed to find the chain unbroken. Lindquist nodded to me and said in a loud voice that I was the best engineer the Old Man had put on the job.

We finished the wheels in a few days, and I was glad, for I wanted to get back on the high iron and I didn't trust the Swede. It was a surprise when he invited me to go fishing with him the next Sunday on the Mohawk. He had a pretty little rowboat painted red with a white stripe around the top and the name *Truda* on the bow, finished with a curlicue at each end that might have been a flower.

As we floated down the river, hugging the bank, ducking under willows and sycamores, looking for riffles, the Swede lounged on the oars with an air of contentment. His hand on the oar was as gentle and soundless as an Indian's, and the color of his variegated whiskers blended with the yellowing leaves. Here he was quiet, and as much a part of the woods and the river as a cow in the meadow or a lichen on a rock. Without turning his head he could detect the slightest movement in the grass or on the water, and in a low voice he told me what it was: a chipmunk under the leaves, a quail rustling the dried grass under a bush, a minnow rising to the surface to snap at a water spider. This was his element; he belonged here, not with the engines and derricks and clanking machinery.

When we had thrown out our lines, Lindquist talked about his boyhood in Sweden, hunting on snowshoes in the winter, fishing and sailing in the summer. Even after he came to America, he must have lived in the open; for he told me about our native fish, how the black bass deposit their spawn in the beds of running streams, and how the females guard the eggs; how the sunfish build little pyramids of stone on which to spawn.

At noon we tied to the bank, Lindquist opened his two-quart pail and I saw that it was completely filled with hard-boiled eggs. He peeled an egg, holding it in his left hand; and with his right, he reached into a vest pocket for salt. When he had sprinkled the egg generously, he popped it whole into his mouth. His Adam's apple quivered, and the egg slid unbroken down his throat. Fascinated, I watched while he swallowed every egg in the pail—telling me between gulps how eels spawn in the deep salt water and the young start their life journey to find fresh water, only to return to the sea to mate and die.

After our Sunday on the river, I knew that in a sense Lindquist was a fake, a gentle creature building himself up as an ogre in the image of the Old Man. But there was no hidden softness about his model. Tom Thatcher was made of granite with a heart of pig iron, and vitriol for blood. Nobody could get the better of him without the aid of a cyclone or some other act of God.

If the Old Man had any softer emotions, he lavished them not on human flesh but on his engines or other mechanical contraptions that caught his fancy. Bicycles were his passion. He always had the newest one, with all the gadgets, and rode it to the enginehouse on Sunday mornings in knee breeches and a tall silk hat—very dignified, inspecting his engines, with never a word for his engineers. It was a sweet moment when he ran into the turntable pit, and Nick Kuhn and I pulled him out, purple with humiliation.

Any sort of engine interested him, especially if it was a neat machine job. For a long time he kept in the storehouse two little steam engines that had been designed to run sewing machines. One of the directors of the road had organized a company to manufacture them and, when the enterprise failed, had given the two models to Tom. He finally sold one for sixty dollars and kept the other as a plaything. It was an ingenious contraption, an eighteen-inch boiler with a neat brass band around it, a little oscillating engine and, for fuel, four kerosene lamps with four flues, all fed from one reservoir.

I never wanted anything so badly as I wanted that little engine, and one day when we were moving the supplies from the old storehouse to the new one about a mile across the yards, I took a chance and lifted it from the Old Man. He hadn't played with it for a long time, and I figured that he had forgotten about it. I was on the yard engine, transferring the stock. During one of the ten- or fifteen-minute waits between runs, while the yardmen were upstairs getting out the stuff for the next load, I posted the fireman to give me a warning toot and smuggled the little engine out through a break in the picket fence. I hid it in the potters' field behind the yard. It weighed about sixty pounds, but I dragged it to the high grass and got back, puffing, as the men finished loading the stuff on the flatcar.

The only place I had to hide my plaything was the basement, and I was afraid mother would smell the kerosene. But she didn't track down the odor when I lit the lamps and got up steam in the little boiler. Twenty pounds she carried, and she puffed away, as sweet as any engine on the line. There was no steam gauge, but I had one made for her.

At the moment the Old Man's attention was completely focussed on the elevator which he had put into the new storehouse. The building was only two stories high, but Tom had the idea that the men couldn't steal so much equipment if they didn't have access to the stairs; so he put in an open cage built after his own design. It was run by a pull rope and stopped by a contrivance that stuck out at the top of the second floor. Perhaps the Old Man calculated originally how much tonnage it would carry, but he was so proud of it that he ended by believing that it would lift anything.

One day when I hauled over a load of "brashes," forty- or fifty-pound bearings for driving-wheels, he ordered us to pile them all on. Old Tom was going up with them, to show Dal Alvord how she worked. Dal, the storekeeper, was a peculiar-looking fellow, with the longest body and the shortest legs I ever saw, and so stupid that you'd hardly expect him to know his own name. Tom hired him because he wasn't a railroad man and had no friends among the crews.

Loaded with Tom and Dal and the brashes, the car labored to the second floor, but when it hit the stopper at the top, it fell back and bumped the starting trigger below with such force that it shot up again.

"Jump, you damned fool, jump," yelled Tom. Dal jumped as the cage descended, and the elevator, lightened by his weight, bounced up again, throwing the Old Man out among the monkey wrenches on the second floor. For a third time the cage fell, this time to the cellar, and imbedded the brashes in the cement.

After his wild ride, Dal refused to touch the elevator; so Old Tom had to get a new storekeeper. When he had a little time to check over his stock, he missed his sewing machine engine and called me in to ask if I had seen it. When I vowed innocence, he said, "I'll tell you what, Joe —you get around among the men. See if you can find out who lifted it. I wouldn't lose that engine for a thousand dollars."

The Old Man made me nervous. If he wanted me to sleuth for him, no telling how many other amateur detectives he had on the job. I began to look for a way to get rid of the engine and hit upon the new storekeeper, who didn't hesitate to take bolts and screws, or whatever he needed in building his new house. He thought the engine sounded wonderful, but he didn't have any cash to give me for it. If I would consider merchandise in trade, he invited me to bring it over and see what I'd like to have.

Eager to get rid of the thing, I dragged it to his house one night. The storekeeper showed me a room full of merchandise—ladies' dresses and petticoats, stockings and all sorts of feminine garments—and urged me to take my pick. His father, he told me, had owned a little drygoods store, and when it failed, he and his mother had saved what they could of the stock.

"You understand," I warned him, "that I just borrowed the engine from the Old Man." Sure, he understood; he was just borrowing it, too, but he intended to play with it for a long time.

When I gave mother two pairs of bright green silk stockings and a pair of red ones, she thought I had lost my mind. "Whatever in the world made you think I'd wear them?" she asked me. "Why, I wouldn't want to be caught dead in them."

I didn't tell her how I got them, and she was suspicious for a long time; but I was relieved to have the engine out of the house. The next time I saw it, the storekeeper had about sixty pounds of steam up, and the boiler looked as if it would burst at any minute. If the Old Man ever saw that engine again, it wouldn't be in one piece.

After a while Old Tom forgot about the engine. He was busy designing an air-compressor to cool the cylinders. It got so hot that it turned red, and the jacket that he built to protect it was always melting off. He could have bought good compressors, but it was against his principles to buy anything that he could make.

Once or twice the Old Man came mighty near to hitting upon a good invention—his movable step for instance, that he attached to a coach and tried out at the passenger station to show the superintendent. It does seem strange that for all these years porters have had to carry little stools to bridge the gap between the first step of the coach and the platform. The Old Man's step was operated by a handle, which shot it out from under the coach step whenever it was needed. It was rickety and awkward, but it worked. The superintendent thought it ought to be patented; and Old Tom began to talk about the money that was in it, if he could get a good man to handle the selling end.

"Mr. Thatcher, I could sell them," I volunteered.

"You? You don't know enough," the Old Man scoffed.

"But you don't need to know anything to sell that," I said. "Only, if I were you, I'd turn the handle down instead of up. Somebody coming down the steps might catch the handle and pull the step under, with him on it." This was the wrong thing to say, for I knew very well that the Old Man didn't like suggestions.

"Don't tell me you thought that up all by yourself! You haven't any brains."

I slunk back to the engine without another word; but I still think that the Old Man had a good idea, although he never did do anything with it.

12. The Great Blizzard

BERT BRYANT, THE FIREMAN ASSIGNED TO me, was a year younger than I. As he had grown up with the railroad, he had no awe of anything, not even Tom Thatcher. He had been firing for his father, one of the best engineers on the road, and looked upon his stint with me as a lark. Bert knew all the shortcuts, and it wasn't long until we were having a picnic on the Old Man's time.

On a day in February—one of those mild interludes when the sun was out, and you could actually smell and feel spring, as soft as plush, under your feet and in the air— Bert began to beat a tattoo on the engine deck with his shovel. The sun was in his blood, and he wanted to go places, dust the coal from his feet and set out for anywhere.

We left Binghamton in the afternoon, wildcatting to Utica with a string of empty boxcars. Before we had swooped around the Grecian Bend, with our headlight picking out the dark arms of the river glimmering between patches of old snow, Bert had an idea: when we got into Utica we could catch the six o'clock morning train to Carthage and spend Sunday with his uncle. I had met his cousins, Walter Bryant and Walter's brother, both engineers on the Black River Line, and knew that his Uncle Spencer was the roadmaster; but Bert held out a special inducement to me: his pretty seventeen-year-old cousin, Mamie. He was sure we could get home on Sunday night, in plenty of time to take a Monday morning call.

It was a couple of hours past midnight when we dropped off our cars in the yard. Bert wanted to paint the stack and leave the engine ready for the Old Man's inspection, so I held the torch while he went across to the paint shop to steal a can of lampblack. In no time we had cleaned out the clinkers, dumped the ashes, painted and oiled and polished, until the engine threw off a fine gleam in the unsteady light. By six o'clock we ourselves were slicked and polished, as well as we could manage it by torch light and in cold water in a tin bucket, and on the train for Carthage.

We had a fine visit with Bert's Uncle Spencer, a big, good-natured Englishman, heavy with dignity. He was from Kent and knew Staplehurst, the home of my father and mother. He remembered the old Norman church with a peep-hole for lepers in the door, and had himself lost two sons in the diphtheria epidemic that took nine of mother's seventeen children. Every Sunday for five weeks, mother had told us, there was a funeral in the house.

Mrs. Bryant, Bert's Irish aunt, let Spencer do the talking, but she was hospitable, and her chicken with hot dumplings spoke louder than a whistle to a couple of hungry boys who had been on the road for nearly three days. Mamie's curly black hair reminded me of Norah's, but her eyes were softer, and when she sang at the parlor organ, her voice was clear and sweet as a catbird's call in the marshes. As I watched her reflection in the mirror set between the little what-not shelves on each side of the high organ, and caught her shy eyes smiling at me, my heart began to do the old painful flop.

When we reached Utica at about midnight on Sunday, pleased with ourselves, we went over to the Lackawanna yards to look at the call board and saw that we were marked up to go out at three that morning. There was also a notice to report at the office on our arrival from Binghamton. In the enginehouse the foreman came over to our track.

"Where have you fellows been?" he demanded. "And what in heck possessed you to paint your engine stack green? I sent a call for you yesterday. Just wait until Old Tom gets you on the carpet."

"Green!" We hadn't noticed. The paint had looked black enough to us by torch light. We had all the way to Binghamton and back to make up a good story; but the longer we thought about it, the more impossible to seemed to find an alibi. There just wasn't any good reason for changing the color of the stack.

When we entered the office, the Old Man stamped to the rail and devoured us with his eye, as if he were contemplating a juicy steak into which he was about to sink his teeth.

"And by whose authority did you change the standard color of the stack on engine 15?"

Speaking softly, I told him how anxious we were to

have our engine look spic-and-span and how we painted it on our arrival, to get the jump on the other crews, and how sorry we were that we got the wrong paint in the dark. The Old Man wasn't listening to a word I said; he was whistling through his teeth, thinking up a string of new swear words. Wheeling on Bert, he thundered: "I had forgotten, Bryant, that you haven't a brain in your head, and it was my mistake to send you out with an engineer who not only has no brains but no place to put them. However, I'll remember you both, when the coal rush is over. Now scat, both of you." He whistled us out the door with a blast of searing curses.

"Whew," groaned Bert, when we got outside in the cool air. "That will hold you the next time you're feeling pretty smart."

The friendship between Bert and me, which the Old Man cemented, held through all the trials of the road, even the great blizzard that we old fellows still talk about when we exchange yarns. We didn't spend four days in the snowbanks digging for rail fences to keep up the steam, or eat our way through a manifest, but we did get our ears nipped and our eyes almost blinded.

On the evening of the big snow, the Old Man sent us to Binghamton with a passenger engine to replace one that had run into the hind end of a coal train and bashed in her front. If we were smart, he said, we could keep on the tail of the late afternoon passenger and get through on her orders; but he didn't want us to overrun any boards. If we lost Number 8, we'd have to wildcat. As it was Saturday, we would have to spend a dull week-end away from home if we missed Number 3, the last passenger out of Binghamton.

When we started at early dusk, it was clear but cold; the damp, bone-chilling cold before a storm. We both hugged the furnace door and kept our eyes fixed on the hind end of Number 8, speeding up when the red balls of her lanterns got small and dim, slowing when they swelled like balloons floating toward us. It was like playing a game with field-glasses, looking first through one end, then the other. We kept close on her tail, crowding her board at the stations and letting out after her on the stretches; but I didn't like the way we were running. The engine was light, and her tall wheels slithered uneasily as if the rails were rubbed with lard. Bert felt it too.

"Dad says greasy rails mean a blizzard," he told me, peering through the front window; but there wasn't a shred of mist, and the farms and haystacks swung into the headlights black and clear.

But when we had climbed over Paris Hill and were coasting down toward the swamp, it began to snow— gently at first, then more steadily, a curtain of dim small flakes that meant a heavy fall. We slowed down. Our headlight was swallowed in the snow, reduced to a pale yellow circle that seemed no bigger than a dollar. We lost the lights of Number 8 and couldn't have seen them unless we were close enough to snub them with the pilot; but we heard her whistle for Sangerfield and followed blindly, creeping up on her just before the board turned red. While the passenger was unloading, the agent came back, with a heavy muffler pulled around his chin and the flakes sticking in blotches to his rusty coat, making him look somehow like a scarecrow. He stood below the cab, holding up his lantern to see my face, and said we were a

couple of crazy fools to try to keep on anybody's tail when we couldn't see a wheel's length before us; but we were pleased with ourselves because we had made the light.

We crept on, trying to keep near enough the passenger to hear her engine, but even the pounding of our own sounded muffled and far away. The wind came up, and the snow began to beat in so hard that we could scarcely breathe. While I strained my eyes against the window, Bert hauled out the side-curtains from the box under my seat and managed to get them up; but even so, the wind billowed them in, spitting gusts of flakes in at the sides.

We nosed straight through Brookfield without even seeing the station, although I did remember vaguely that we had a green light. Hours later, it seemed, I could tell by the pull of the engine as we took the hump that we had come to Hubbardsville. The light was green; Number 8 had given us the slip and was so far ahead that the board had changed. The stationmaster was waving us a lowball with the lantern, no more than a red pinpoint swinging back and forth. He came out of the white froth and shouted to us that we had orders to hole up for the fast freight. Number 8 had a meet with it at Pooleville. This was not a night telegraph station. Generally he locked the doors at five o'clock, and he was as grouchy as a setting hen.

We crunched into the siding and waited. The blanket of snow on the steel roof steamed as it melted, and the cab was hot and suffocating. Bert stripped off his jacket and looked at his watch—nine o'clock already. We hadn't a snail's chance of catching Number 3. To kill time, Bert pulled a grubby pack of cards out of his jacket and dealt them on his seat, pretending to tell our fortunes. After a while we began to talk about what we intended to do. Bert wanted to go west, where a fellow had space to let an engine out. These little roads in the East were too cramped, he said—just a few hundred miles long, with a way station around every curve; but on a run from Chicago to San Francisco, you'd have a chance to see what an engine could do. I settled for a crack train on the old Lackawanna, snaking around the riffles of the Chenango, where you could almost reach out of the cab and pick the foxgloves and ladyslippers in the spring, and could smell the wild honeysuckle for miles—that, and Mamie waiting for me in a pretty little white house like Gander Schnell's, putting on the potatoes when she heard my whistle on Schuyler Street. What did he think about Mamie? Did I have a chance with her?

Bert nodded his head. He thought I stood ace high with Mamie, and Uncle Spencer was all right; but I'd have a difficult time with Aunt Sarah. She would never want her baby to live as far away from home as Utica. He promised to take me to Carthage every Sunday that we could get away.

The snow kept spluttering past the edges of the curtains—not the driving flurries that whipped in whenever we were moving, but enough to make us dust ourselves off every few minutes and to cover the deck with slush. We began to be hungry. Both of us had eaten before we started, expecting to get a plate of ham and eggs at Binghamton and have breakfast at home in Utica; but when a man is sitting cooped up helpless in a storm, he begins to think of the things he'd like to eat. Bert was getting restless. He wanted to plow across to the station and find out what was going on. I was anxious for a little action too, so I promised to watch the fire until he came back.

After what seemed hours, he pulled up the handrail, thrusting his neck and shoulders into the cab—a living snowman, every inch of him, even his eyelashes covered with the clinging stuff. He gave me a start, for I hadn't heard the crunch of his feet. Every sound except the wind was swallowed up in the snow. He shook himself in the tender and came in with a tin of coffee in his hand.

"Here, drink this. Tom gave me a cup. He says there's going to be an unholy mess on the road, and here's an order. He let me sign for it." Bert held up the lantern while I read. Something had happened to the through freight between here and Pooleville. We were to nose along down the road and see what we could do to get her into Hubbardsville or back her up to Pooleville and clear the track. Bert crawled out to see that our taillights were burning (not that they did much good), and I wiped off the headlight. The steam kept our front window clear, but the headlight was so faint that it barely lit the pilot.

After we had inched into the smother for half an hour or so, straining through the window until our eyes were red, Bert grabbed my arm. At the same moment we caught the red point of a lantern. I threw the lever into the big hole, and we both climbed out.

A brakeman with a scarf tied over his mouth and chin motioned us to follow him. We couldn't see the freight but came upon it in a few steps. Red Strothers, the engineer, and his fireman were on the ties, wallowing around with wrenches and crowbars, while a couple of shacks held lanterns in their faces. Red got to his feet and peered at us.

"That you, Joe? What are you and Bert doing, wild-catting around on a night like this? We've thrown a right main spring. You should have seen the fire spurting out of the mud ring into this lather—looked like the Fourth of July. We're just outside of Poole. Think you could back us into the siding?"

I nodded. His hind shack hung onto the back of the caboose, ready to throw the switch.

"Squeeze into the cab, boys," Red said. "Your fire's gone out in the caboose and there ain't no use freezing to death trying to decorate the top."

We plowed back to our engine and eased her forward, watching the red lantern of the shack, who stood by, waiting to tie us on. The freight was a heavy push for a light buggy, even if the track had been clear; but after a try or two we got her rolling, heaved her into the siding and edged her nose past the main iron. The station was dark and locked. Red said he would be all right. If they couldn't patch the spring they would hole up for the night. They had plenty of coal and could use the snow to keep up steam, and if they got too hungry, they would break into the manifest. We pushed on and, by some miracle of good luck, got a clear board to Norwich. It was next to impossible to see the lights, but we knew where they were and got out to look.

At Norwich we waited for not more than twenty min-utes—long enough to grab a couple of doughnuts and a cup of coffee from old Santa Claus. The operator was looking grim when we reported that the freight was holed up at Pooleville, and he shut off the instrument long enough to call our orders.

"Go ahead to the Forks, but be sure and check there. Here," he handed us a blue order, "and don't let in the whole Arctic Circle when you open the door."

We steamed along, mile after mile, with the same gray wall ahead, giving before us and closing in on our tail—climbing out to look at the boards, guessing where we were by the humps and curves in the road. Fool's luck got us to Binghamton that night. I spotted the engine on the pit and tore off my orders, while Bert looked around to see if anything was moving toward Utica. We were both determined to get back unless we had to walk. He found that Number 3 was just about to pull out. It had waited to follow an engine with a steel wedge plow clamped to the pilot, which was going to try to keep open the cut not far beyond Greene. A freight was stalled on the siding there, and if the plow could open up the way, both it and the passenger would probably get through to Utica. As we went back to Number 3, we passed the improvised snow plow on the ready track, an engine with a caboose piled full of shovels and a crew sitting on the floor around a little pot-bellied stove with a can of coffee on it.

As we were climbing into the hind coach of Number 3, the engine foreman grabbed Bert and put him on to fire the snow plow. He made a glum face at me as he back-tracked to the other train.

We crept along, not too close to the snow plow. The train was almost empty, with only the crew and a handful of passengers, mostly Utica business men who were determined to get home before they were snowed in. Every once in a while, when the engineer stopped to look at a board, the conductor got out and knuckled his wheels to see if they were hot, or one of the brakemen shoveled snow into the boiler.

Willie, the flagman, was a boomer who cursed his luck, thinking of Florida. He had been south the year before, and as he sat in on our game of poker, he told us about his trip to Georgia in the spring of '86. On that famous May Sunday when every railroad in the South changed its wide gauge to standard, he had sat in a caboose on a stretch of Atlantic Coast line and watched the gandy dancers ripping up the rail on one side of the track and resetting it three inches and a half nearer the other. From dawn to sunset they sweated and grunted, racing along the line, and by dark every road in the South was remade: any coach in the United States could go from Maine to California or New Orleans. That was the life, Willie said, getting around and seeing things; only it was getting harder and harder with the Master Mechanics and train-masters kicking a man about as if he were a common tramp.

At Greene the boomer and I got off and tramped forward in a smother of blinding snow, to watch the plow at work. It ran into the cut, then backed a half mile and shot forward again, the throttle wide open, bucking into the cushion of snow that brought it to a stop without putting on the brakes. The engineer threw her into reverse, pulled her free, and bucked again, while the crew held on to each other and cheered as the snow cascaded onto the roof of the quivering caboose.

When the plow broke through, we went back to Number 3 that followed close behind her until she took the siding at Brisben and tooted us on our way. The rest of the night we inched along, and when morning finally came, the light made very little difference in the visibility. About noon we dragged into the Utica yards, cramped and half starved, and faced the problem of getting home. I lived only a few blocks away, but it took all the strength I had left to pull my feet out of snow as high as my knees. Number 3 was the last train that got through until after the big snow.

By Monday morning the blizzard was at its height. There were no deliveries, no milk, no groceries, and the fences were down. I knew that no train could go out in this storm, even if I could break through to the yards; so I played cards with mother, fried eggs, ate her good home-made bread and drank black coffee.

By Friday I decided it was time to get back to the roundhouse. The snow was over, and the plows had opened up the main streets; so I shoveled a path to the road, curious to know what had happened to the rest of the crews. As a precaution against the Old Man, I asked mother to sew a strip of red flannel around my neck, as if I had sore throat.

"Oh, I wouldn't do that, Joe," mother said, but she found a piece of flannel and sewed it on for me.

Outside the office I met Rogers, who told me that the trains were just beginning to get through. One or two had come in that morning. Lindquist was at the cut with the snow plow, had been there for a couple of days; an engine had overturned in the snow; one crew of a passenger had lived high and fed themselves on the perishable stuff in the express car, cooking in the firebox.

While we stood there, the Old Man came out of the office with his high boots on, carrying a shovel. Pushing his way through a crowd of section hands, Italians with blue ears and noses who had been working all night, he stamped ahead as if he were going to shovel the whole road himself.

"Keep out of here, keep out of here," he bellowed when he saw me. "I'm sick and tired of men coming in here groaning. I'll give you double time." He nodded to Rogers, who went in and entered it in the big book.

When the Old Man got out of the way, I went to the roundhouse to see if Bert had come in and found him playing seven-up with the fireman and a couple of shacks from Number 3. When he heard that the Old Man had given me double time, he whistled with admiration. I promised to split with him, and we decided to cash in on the future. It was two weeks before the ghost walked, but between us we could advance ourselves enough to splurge in Carthage on Sunday. Bert promised to write Mamie that very afternoon. I knew just the box of candy to take her: a big, red, heart-shaped box of chocolates that I had seen in a shop window, with lace around the edges like a valentine, tied with red ribbon three or four inches wide. Valentine's Day was past, but hearts, I figured, were always in season.

At the end of the next week we went to Carthage, spending our velvet in advance; but when the ghost walked I got the double pay. None of the crew of Number 3 tattled, and the Old Man didn't know until years later that I had beaten him out of eight days' pay.

13. The Grievance Committee

OON AFTER MY PROMOTION I JOINED THE Brotherhood of Locomotive Engineers— the Binghamton Division, because the B. of L. E. was a rag even redder to the Old Man than the Firemen's union. He had fought it so bitterly that it was not yet very strong or well organized in Utica. Only about half of us belonged. The others were, in railroad parlance, "no bills."

The union was an old one. It had been organized thirty-odd years earlier by a group of midwestern engineers—august, long-bearded doubles for the Smith Brothers—who had fought hard for the betterment of the service. The Brotherhood had been the goad that led to the establishment of the Interstate Commerce Commission and the adoption of the safety appliances which, one after the other, have reduced the hazards of railroading. In those days a man was killed on an average of every two hours, and one injured every twenty minutes.

Just the year before, the new automatic coupler that the switchman could release from the side of the track had been made mandatory by the Commission, and the roads were given two years in which to install new equipment: no more pin couplings to catch the brakeman's fingers. In a few years you wouldn't be able to spot a brakeman by his mutilated hand. The fight for the adoption of air brakes was on, and already the old jimmies with their punishing high side-brakes were obsolete.

When I joined, the Brotherhood was involved in a strike on the C. B. & Q. Very few of our men went out, but we supported it to the limit with our pay. Fourteen dollars out of my month's slim wages went into the war chest; but I considered it well spent, because I was beginning to realize that the Brotherhood was fighting for me. I was quite sure that Mamie wouldn't like to be torn up from a pretty little house in Utica (the house that I was already furnishing in my mind) and dumped at a new terminal in some godforsaken field, miles from friends and stores and churches.

As the roads expanded, shooting their lines farther and farther into new territory, they set up their shops and offices wherever the tracks came to an end and dragged the crews and their families along unnecessarily, with no consideration of the human needs of their men. Our road was fairly stable, but there was no telling what day the management might decide to branch off toward the St. Lawrence and move us all away from Utica.

Being an ardent young member of the Brotherhood was fair enough, but being an official with the job of facing the Old Man was a horse of another color. One day when I came into the roundhouse to take out an extra passenger, Scotty, one of the older engineers on the coal, said to me, "Joe, you've been elected to the Grievance Committee."

I wasn't too pleased. It was one of those honors that you'd rather see lighting on somebody else.

"Now, Joe," Scotty remonstrated, "don't look like that. Somebody's got to take it. You're a single man and young. The Old Man knows that you can get another job any day of the week." I pointed out to him that I was taking care of my mother and just as good as married—would be married, I added to myself, if Mamie would say the word. But he wouldn't take no.

"It won't be so tough, Joe," he promised. "All you've got to do is to see that the men get a square deal. The Old Man doesn't have investigations when there are accidents, and he's got to have them. If he gets too hot, you can just go in and talk to him. He hasn't any right to swear at the boys and throw things at them. They don't do that sort of thing these days."

Reluctantly I accepted, and began to dread to come to work each morning for fear something had happened that would require my appearance before the Old Man. But the days slipped by uneventfully, the snow melted and the lady-slippers came out along the river; and nearly every Sunday Bert and I hopped a train of the Black River Line and deadheaded to Carthage with one of the cousins.

We were always welcome at his uncle's house. The fried chicken or goose or turkey, stuffed with chestnuts, filled the kitchen with a tantalizing aroma, and the big walnut cake with white icing stood under the glass cake plate on the sideboard. I followed Mamie around like a Newfoundland pup, getting in the way when she set the table, trying to help her with the dishes. Affairs were going well with us; but "Aunt Sarah" (as I called her mother), although not inhospitable, took care never to leave us alone. In a quiet way she was like a stone wall set against me; not all of my blarney could move her an inch. Even Bert had no better luck in trying to get her out of the way. Still, eyes talk when there is no opportunity for words.

Maybe in time I could win over Aunt Sarah. Anyway Mamie loved me, and that was what mattered. Life was running along on golden wheels, and I paid no heed to any thought of trouble. I even looked proudly at my name listed in the minutes of the Brotherhood as Chairman of the Grievance Committee. Some time later in the summer, when the moment did come, I was feeling so pleased with myself that I actually stuck my head into the noose.

One morning when I got to the enginehouse early to take out my train, I met Henry Wilson, a big, inarticulate fellow who was a runner on the local freight. Henry was looking as if he had seen the devil. When I asked him what was the matter, he told me that on the run from Binghamton the night before, a journal on the end of an axle had burnt off the tank of his engine and the Old Man had sent for him.

"He'll eat the face off me, Joe, and when he goes at me, I just fill up and can't say a thing."

"Henry," I said, sticking out my chest, "the Old Man will have to give you a fair hearing and no cussing. I'll take up the case with him. We'll go in and face him. You say 'Good morning,' as if nothing had happened; then I'll take over. Don't get angry and lose your temper."

Bert, who had come in with a pint of oil and a handful

of new waste that he had lifted from the storeroom, let out a raucous cheer.

"Atta big boy. Wipe up the Old Man." Everybody else in the shop gathered around. They slapped me on the back, shook hands and, groaning mournfully, pulled out their handkerchiefs and pretended to dab their eyes. Even the foreman looked after me with a malicious grin.

"Come on, Henry," I said loftily, trying to bolster up my dignity. By the time we reached the office door, I felt more like Daniel saying "pretty kitty" to the lions than I did like a Committeeman. As we passed the window, we looked in, to size up the situation. If the Old Man was smoking, it wouldn't be so bad; but he was bending over the desk, writing in a ledger.

"He nearly brained Scotty last week with a paperweight, when Scotty asked for a new cushion for the cab," muttered Henry. I glowered at him. There was no use hanging around outside, especially with the boys in the enginehouse keeping their eyes on us. Hat in hand, we went in and stood by the railing in front of the Old Man's desk.

"Good morning, Mr. Thatcher," said Henry in a faint voice, no louder than a whisper. Old Tom looked up.

"Good morning, God damn ye!"

Going at once into high gear, as he always did at these sessions, he asked the questions and answered them himself.

"And what do you mean by burning off a tank journal? You came all the way from Binghamton to Utica without putting a drop of oil on your engine. Too lazy to get off your backside—too lazy to look out of the window. This journal was afire for miles. You could have smelled it if you had put that dog-face out of the window. You might have killed somebody, destroyed thousands of dollars worth of property. To think that I have had an engineer for eight long years without a brain in his head."

"But, Mr. Thatcher, the journal didn't burn off, it twisted off."

"Don't come to me with a lie on your lips." As the Old Man sputtered to himself, gaining momentum for a new string of oaths, he wheeled his head and his good eye lit on me.

"And what are you doing here?" he shouted.

Flushing to my ears, I answered, "I'm the Committeeman."

Old Tom let out a bellow that was intended for a laugh.

"My God, Rogers," he said to the clerk, "look at the Committeeman. Outside, loafers! Sneak thieves!" He reached over the desk, blindly feeling for something to throw, but Henry and I were moving, and we didn't stop until we reached the other side of the Goose Pasture. When Henry stopped panting, he turned on me indignantly.

"My God, Joe, you're a hell of a Committeeman."

"But, Henry," I tried to argue, "you ran out before I had a chance to cut loose. And you must remember I had to treat the Old Man with respect. Anyway, I didn't get riled."

"What do you mean, I left first!" Henry said. "You were ahead of me, and I saw you take that five-foot fence with a good two feet to spare." It was pretty hard to go back to the enginehouse and face the boys, but they were fairly evenly divided as to which one got over the fence first. We both went out on our runs as usual and said no more about it, but I never could convince Henry that my clever work had got him out of trouble.

Luckily, nobody needed my services during the rest of the summer, and my own affairs kept me so busy that there was no time to brood over my inglorious performance as a Committeeman. I was getting nowhere with Aunt Sarah. Bert was urging direct action, but I didn't want to antagonize her family. Autumn dragged along in a stalemate, until one evening at John Collins' I met Walter, Mamie's brother, in off his run, and asked him what he thought about the situation.

"Mother likes you all right," he said, "but she doesn't want Mamie to leave home. She's unreasonable that way—wants to keep her hands on all of us. She queered me with a couple of girls, and I don't want to see the same thing happen to Mamie."

"What do you think I ought to do?" I asked.

He promised to visit his aunt in Rome the first Sunday he had a chance. She might be persuaded to say that she was ill and needed Mamie to stay with her for a couple of weeks. This he could do; the rest was up to Mamie and me.

Just after Christmas I got a note from Mamie saying that she was going to Rome for a visit. On January sixteenth we were married, and I took Mamie to Utica, to the house that had been home to my mother and me for so many years. Mother, who wisely felt that two young people in love could make a better start together without the supervision of their elders, paid a long-contemplated visit to England.

Now I was a married man with a wife to support, and plenty of responsibility. No more skylarking with Bert, fooling around and taking chances; no more stealing time from the Old Man. But I counted without Bert, who had no intention of letting Mamie blight our good times, just because she happened to marry me. Indeed, he felt that the match was his idea in the first place and would never have come off without his masterly assistance; so he made it the occasion for a celebration that lasted several months.

The affair of the Unadilla Valley Railroad was one of our final pranks. The dairy business around Richfield Springs had begun to assume importance to the roads. The Lackawanna had put on a daily milk train; and a group of financiers in New York were opening up new dairy country with the Unadilla Valley Railroad, twenty-two miles of road that connected with the Lackawanna at Bridgewater, the first stop beyond the Junction on the line to Richfield Springs. Six miles of the line had been built, and the officials were coming to inspect it. Their private car was attached to Number 3, which Bert and I were running in from Binghamton. It was to be picked up at Utica and taken to Bridgewater by another engine.

Every time we made a stop, Johnny, the flagman who rode in the rear car with all the grandeur, came forward and told us what a high time the officials were having; there was not a sober one among them. At Richfield Junction he reported that the chef was serving quail on toast and that champagne was flowing like water.

"Champagne?" questioned Bert, with a gleam in his eye. "What do you suppose it tastes like, Joe?" Luckily we had to pull out, for I could see that Bert had mischief in his head.

When we got into the station at Utica, the superintendent came to the cab and told me not to back up the train until he had corralled the Unadilla Railroad people, who were swarming all over the place. Bert and I dropped off and went back to take a look. The shack was right; they were having a happy time. The private car had a balcony on the hind end, with an iron railing, and just inside the railing was a big box filled with straw.

"That's it," whispered Bert. "I've heard it comes in straw. Let's lift a couple of bottles." I shook my head. "Oh, come on," he urged. "The fast freight is due on the New York Central." (The tracks were very near the Lackawanna at this point.) "It makes such a racket that nobody will hear us. I'll climb up and hand you down a couple of bottles, and you skin for the engine."

"Not me," I said, but as he started to pull himself up by the rail, I jerked him back. I was taller and older than he, and if anyone was going to do it, I stood a better chance. I skinned up the railing, stuck my hand into the straw, grabbed a couple of bottles and jumped as the freight came by. We loped back to the engine and hid the bottles with the links and waste and pins in a supply box in the back of the truck.

Before we returned to the cab, a porter came along in

a white coat, shouting for the engineer. I leaned out and asked him what was up. Mr. Culver, the president of the Unadilla road, wanted to see me in the private car. The darkie turned with the haughty dignity that can be achieved only by the porter of a private car, and I followed him along the ties with my heart beating a nervous tattoo against my ribs.

A group of men was sitting around three or four tables in the dining end of the car, already covered with half-filled glasses and elaborately set with silver. One of them smiled at me and invited me to sit down.

"You have made a very nice run," he said. "We want to give you a good dinner." Stammering with relief, I managed to thank them and decline, explaining that my wife was waiting for me.

"Then take a little something to drink," they urged. I regretted that I was still on duty.

"George," called Mr. Culver, "bring the gentleman a bottle of champagne to take home." While George went to the box on the balcony, icicles pricked my spine. Would he notice that two bottles were gone? But he came back looking as inscrutable as ever, with the bottle wrapped in straw. My pockets stuffed with fine cigars and the bottle under my arm, I went front and climbed on the engine, feeling very small.

Meanwhile Bert had passed the word around, and when we got to the yard, Paddy Kelly, who was going to take the car out to Bridgewater, said that if I could steal one, he could. He and Bert wouldn't wait until they got home to open their bottles but pulled the corks in the coal shed.

I took a taste of theirs. It was wonderful stuff, but I took mine home to Mamie. When she looked me in the eye and said, "You're late. What made you lose time?" I pulled out one bottle, and we drank it for supper, pretending it was our wedding supper, both very happy. The other bottle we kept for many years.

Luckily for our peace of mind, Bert soon hopped a high-ball freight and went west, where a man could stretch himself and let his engine out. He became one of the best-known engineers on the Chicago & Rock Island Railroad and ran the Golden Gate Limited for fourteen years. All the Bryants were first-class railroad men.

14. The Runaway Train

GRADUALLY I WAS BEGINNING TO LOSE THE resemblance to a hop pole that had made Boney and Henry Millgate regard me with misgivings. Better padding on my lanky bones made me look more like a responsible married man and an engineer; but I yearned for two things to complete the picture: a handlebar mustache and a dog to ride in the engine with me.

The idea of the mustache I finally abandoned; it was no use trying, I never could raise one. But of the dog I had stronger hopes. Ever since I had valeted old Phil Doubleday's Fly, filling his water tin that sat in a corner of the Butterfly's cab under the right-hand seat and stealing waste to make him a bed, I had regarded a dog as the perquisite of an engineer—like the top-floor-front rooms of the Globe Hotel (the ones with the wardrobes in them) and the front tables at John O'Brien's saloon.

Shorty Burns, one of the best engineers on the coal trains, had a little honey-colored spaniel named Rags that looked just like him, except she wasn't quite so fat. Shorty stood less than five feet and was wider around; but for all that, he was an impressive figure, and almost as much of a dude as old Baldy, with his spotless white shirts, his big cigars and his curly red hair and whiskers perfumed with musk.

Rags rode under Shorty's seat, except when she retired for a few weeks in the summer to present him with a family. If I had one of Rags' puppies, a dog born to the tradition of the rails, to keep me company, I felt that life would be complete; but Shorty wouldn't promise definitely. He said that Rags always had the final say in the disposition of her children, and he wasn't sure that she liked me.

There wasn't much opportunity to make up to Rags; we weren't often in the yards together. But one Saturday night, when Shorty and I were both eager to get our drags to Utica and knock off for the week-end, she gave me her approval. My train, which had Gander Schnell as conductor, had dropped three gondolas of coal at Norwich for the New York, Ontario & Western. When we cut out four, we could get over the hill without doubling; but I doubted if Gander would let us try it with three. It was dark when we slid down the grade into the flat stretch at Waterville, where we cleaned the fire for the hill. Shorty was ahead of us, and he was out of sight.

Gander came front and said, "Shorty's going to get over the hill without doubling. If we can catch him, try to hook on to him without letting him know it, and we'll both get over."

Pulling out of Waterville, I began to lace the engine. I'd have to hop it through the cut and tie on to him before we came to Marshall's crossing; for that was my last chance to double if we didn't couple into him. Gander stayed on the engine and watched as we shot around the first curve, and he saw Shorty's red lights going into the cut.

"Put out your headlights, Joe," said Gander. "Old Shorty won't know you're on."

The shack put out the light, but we were going pretty fast. It would be ticklish driving to get slowed down enough to keep from ramming him, then regulate to his speed and creep up without giving him a jar. The flagman on the caboose in front saw what I was doing; when we got within a few feet of him, I could see the man hanging out, waiting, with a coupling pin.

Old Gander was standing there, tense as a pointer. The fireman was holding his breath, and so was I. So too, you would almost think, was the engine; for if we hit the caboose too hard, we would smash it into kindling wood. We were within three feet of the red lights, then two. I shut down the steam to a whisper, and we eased up and kissed the caboose as gently as if it had been a baby. The shack dropped in the pin, and Gander relaxed and squirted a stream of tobacco juice out the window. The fireman opened the firebox door to throw in coal, not afraid now that Shorty might see the glow in the sky.

Opening up, I gave the engine all the power she would take. We weren't free riders; we were going to push with every ounce of steam the old girl had. When we stopped at Paris, on top of the hill, Shorty climbed down and walked back along the track, followed by Rags, stretching her legs.

"Well, I'll be jim-whiskered," said Shorty when he saw us. "I couldn't tell what the devil made the train draw so hard, and when I looked back, I couldn't think what made it so long." Rags who was paying no attention to any of them, came over and licked my hand.

"The gal seems right proud of you. I guess you get one of the pups," Shorty said. A week later he invited me to his house, and I picked out a six-month-old pup, Tim—a lively little fellow, with his mother's coloring and the shorter legs of an unknown father.

Mamie fed Tim and trained him until he was house-broken and ready for railroad life. Then I dressed him up in a collar and led him to the yards on a string. For the first trip, I thought it well to tie the pup to the lever, and made him a soft bed under the seat. He quivered when I opened the cylinder cocks, and when the pistons began to pick up speed, I patted his head reassuringly; but when I whistled at Schuyler Street crossing, he snapped the string and jumped out of the engine with an unholy wail.

Bert doubled with laughter, but I grieved for Tim. That was the last we ever saw of him. Mamie asked all the children along Schuyler Street, but none of them had seen a frightened, honey-colored hound with bandy legs. After that, I never tried to take another dog on the engine.

That autumn, when Bert left for Chicago, the Old Man gave me Jim Fancy for a fireman. Jim was green; he couldn't read or sign his name in the pay book. But he was one of the most magnificent human specimens that I have seen in nearly eighty years. I came upon him first in the Goose Pasture, where we were loading scrap—Lindquist and his gang and, for some reason, the Old Man. After the scrapped cars were burned, the castings lay around until there was a carload or two of them to send to Scranton. They were heavy hunks of iron, these castings (some of them weighed several hundred pounds), but the Old Man never used the derrick when he could do the work by man-power.

I leaned out of the cab window to watch them shout at hunkies trying to heave a center casting into the flatcar, but they couldn't lift it; not even with the advice of the Old Man, bellowed from the sidelines. Pat Kelly, the section foreman, was watching too, with a complacent grin on his face.

"A fine lot of hunkies you have, trying to put in a little casting like that," he said to Tom. "I have a man working across the yard who can put it in alone."

"Like hell you have. Bring him here and let me see him do it."

"Sure I will." Pat bawled across the yard: "Jim! Jim Fancy!"

Jim came from the other side of the Goose Pasture, walking lightly, quick and graceful as a cat—all full six feet of him smooth, well-padded muscle, with not an ounce of extra flesh. His red hair was so alive that you would have expected it to strike sparks if you touched it. He had blue-green eyes set far apart, his face was dusted with freckles and his bare arms covered with a red fuzz that rippled like a wheat field in a breeze. He wore nothing but shoes and a pair of trousers, and even these seemed out of place on his perfect body. Not one of us said a word.

"Jim," said Kelly, "put that casting in the car for Mr. Thatcher. Get a good hold on it now. Breast high. Heave, oh *heave*." Jim leaned over, lifted the casting and as Kelly shouted the last "heave," tossed it on the car.

"That's all, Jim. Thank you." Fancy nodded and went back to his work as if he had done nothing more remarkable than hoisting a toothpick. The Old Man and Lindquist stared at each other in disbelief. Finally Tom found his voice.

"Who is that fellow, Kelly? Call him back. I'll give him a job firing." Jim came back and accepted the Old Man's offer with no particular enthusiasm. The next morning he was assigned to me on a coal train.

"Good morning, Mr. Bromley," he said. "Will you tell me what to do?"

That was the first time anyone had called me "mister." I was so pleased and startled, felt so benevolent toward Jim, that I immediately began to take a hand in civilizing him.

Jim was going to make a first-rate fireman—that I could see. Every movement was easy and precise. He handled the lumps of coal, bigger than watermelons, as if they were peas, and seemed to know intuitively how to make a fire. But in spite of my fatherly attitude, he made me nervous. There was an impersonal power about him, like the wheels of a mighty sawmill that would cut you to ribbons if you got in their way, or an engine running wide open down a hill. When he opened the firebox door, the glow lighting up his naked chest and shoulders, made them look like bronze.

Puzzled about Jim, I tried to find out how he lived and what sort of family he had. When we holed up at the way stations, he never hung around the switch and played cards with the shacks or looked up a saloon to find a glass of beer. He disappeared in the woods and came back when I whistled him in. The other men looked at him curiously, but they never made fun of him. One didn't laugh at Jim.

He could imitate the caw of the crow, the trill of the meadowlark or the three brisk notes of the quail, and he could catch fish with his bare hand, standing motionless in the river and scooping them up as I have seen a bear do it. In the woods he moved without a sound. Sometimes I went with him into the swamp, but he could lose me in a few minutes. After I floundered around a bit, I would hear a thrush in the bushes and look to see Jim's head sticking out of a thicket, grinning at me.

One Saturday afternoon when Jim said he was deadheading to Waterville to go hunting, I went along. The boys at the enginehouse waved me off with hoots of derision, for although I was an average shot, dead-eye Jim was the most famous hunter in the valley. We climbed off of a coal train at Waterville and headed for the swamp. Jim told me to take one side of the woods and he would work the other, skirting the edge, where the birds liked to perch in the sun, avoiding the twilight of the deep woods.

After he disappeared, I tramped through the briars and clumps of birches, keeping moving, hoping to flush a covey of partridges; but I walked for a long time without seeing a single bird. When the sun got hot, I sat on a fallen log to rest, and after my eyes grew accustomed to the dappled pattern of the leaves, I distinguished a partridge sitting on a low branch of a thicket. It wasn't good sportsmanship to shoot a bird at rest, but I was ashamed to go back with nothing; so I took careful aim and got the bird, a plump hen that would make a good mouthful in a pie.

When I had walked for an hour without another shot, I turned back toward the station and in a little natural clearing came upon a farm boy with a shotgun and a bag of game.

"Any luck?" I asked.

"Oh, some." He showed me three woodcock.

"Want to sell them?"

He said he didn't mind, so I added them to the partridge and thought what a grand joke I'd have on Jim Fancy when he saw my bag. Coming to a shady clump of rocks by a brook, it occurred to me that I ought to sit down and wait a little while. Jim would never be taken in if I came back too soon with a string of cold birds. As I rested against the moss, a big cottontail rabbit hopped out of the high meadow grass and stopped to nibble a plantain leaf. Leaning over quietly, I picked up my gun and got a good bead on him.

With this impressive bag, I edged around the swamp to our meeting-place and found Jim Fancy waiting for me under our appointed sycamore. He was sitting on a log, motionless beside a clump of wild blue asters, and his bag was flat as a pancake. It was no fun to make a joke of my good shooting when he was empty-handed, so I offered to divide my birds; but he gave me a scornful look from those frosty green eyes and refused to take even one. When we got back to Utica, the joke was on me, for the boys wouldn't believe that Jim Fancy hadn't given me the birds.

Although there wasn't a rock or a stump in the whole valley that Jim didn't know, his actual home was in Clayville, a village a few miles from Richfield Junction. There he had grown up with his father in a cabin in the woods, hunting, fishing, trapping for the few supplies that they needed from the stores. In England, he told me, his father had been a great poacher, and he was even more successful in this country, with more woods and greater freedom. Jim had never been to school nor worn a shirt.

When Jim had been with me about three weeks we saw the red flag on the pilot of the morning train.

"The ghost will walk tomorrow," I told him. "When you get your pay, I want you to come with me and buy yourself a shirt and a new suit of clothes. And you can get a regular boardinghouse, too. It isn't good for you to sleep around in the cabooses or anywhere you can find, and eat from hand to mouth."

Jim indicated that these suggestions were all right with him, all except the shirt. He thought that this was a peck of foolishness; but I persuaded him that if he would learn to read and write and pay more attention to his clothes, he could qualify in a few years as an engineer.

The day after the ghost walked, we got our drag in early, and I went downtown with Jim to buy the clothes. He had saved twenty-five dollars at my suggestion, and we picked out a good tan suit that looked well with his hair and his gray-green eyes, a shirt, a hat and a new pair of shoes. Although they were good clothes, I was disappointed in the effect of all this finery; somehow the clothes seemed to dull him. But I continued to encourage him, for if he wanted to get anywhere, he must learn to wear a shirt and tie.

"Now, Jim," I urged him, "dress up on Sunday afternoon and come down to the enginehouse like the rest of the boys. I want them to see how good you look." He came, but I was denied my satisfaction for he was wearing the suit without a shirt, and he hadn't shaved.

The rest of his money he kept until the next week-end, when he went home to Clayville for a good time. He was back on Monday morning, tousled and surly, reeking with whisky. I got him out before the Old Man saw him and trusted that the booze would wear off before he got back. The drink had no effect upon his coordination, and he stoked the fire with the same easy precision, but between times he slumped drowsily on his seat.

After a few weeks I could see that the work was boring Jim. It was too easy. He wanted something to happen, something that tested his strength or made his blood tingle with a sense of danger. He had an inarticulate contempt for the engine, because he had to feed it, and hadn't tried to drive it; he didn't know the thrill of feeling it respond under the hand. Once only I saw him moved with a kinship for it: the time we rode down the hill on a runaway train.

We were pulling Gander Schnell and a coal drag when

it happened. I had never quite forgotten the first time I was sent out with Gander after my promotion. I had Old Mike for fireman. He was an engineer who had been set back. One eye was blind, put out by an ammonia bottle thrown playfully in a fight, and he was too feeble to be shoveling coal. Gander, who was doubtful about me, suggested that I let Mike take the throttle going up the hill, but I would have died of shame.

"Keep your nose out of this. I'll run the engine," I said icily to Gander, and he retired to the caboose, a bit disgruntled. But by the time we got in, he had forgiven me and told the Old Man that I had made a fine run.

This night, as we were standing at Richfield Junction with a heavy drag of gondolas for Utica, Gander told me that the speed recorder wasn't working in the caboose. If we let them dance a little, we could make Utica before our orders expired. To make sure, he said he would let them down himself. Letting a heavy train down a steep grade by hand brakes was no job for a novice, but if anybody could do it, Gander was the man. Anyway, I was a young pup, in no position to question the conductor, who was boss of the train.

"Give them a start, kid," he said as we pulled out, "and leave the rest to me." I gave the engine some steam to get us rolling, pushed in the throttle, and we started downhill, picking up speed. The tender began to weave from side to side, and I had an uneasy feeling that we were scooting on greased rails. The wheels weren't even turning over. When we hit Clayville, I knew we were going too fast, but I had no control of the train. Jim Fancy had begun to notice the speed. He was on his feet leaning out the window, his face aglow with excitement.

As we shot through Saquoit, I bit my tongue until it was sore, determined not to show the white feather; but as we rocked into New Hartford, I could stand it no longer. A half mile on the other side was the West Shore crossing. We were supposed to come to a full stop, but we were gaining speed. My hand gripped the whistle cord and gave a shriek for brakes. I prayed that the signal would show green, and it did; but we couldn't have stopped if it had been red. I kept jerking the whistle, calling for brakes, but Gander paid no attention. Jim looked at me derisively, his mouth parted and his eyes gleaming.

"Get out and help," I shouted to him, half choked with rage and fear. He went back and stood by the tender brake with his pick handle in his fist, but he made no move to turn the wheel. He swayed with the engine as we hit the curves. We tipped so far that I thought we would surely leave the track.

"Pray, you fool!" I shouted. "Pray. This is your last run!" But he did not hear me, he was in a trance: quivering, exalted. Bitterly I took my eyes away from him and stared through the front window.

The New York, Ontario & Western crossing came next, but the traffic was light and we leaped across on a green. I caught one glimpse of peglegged Herman Crouse waving his lantern at us, his eyes bulging with astonishment. I was still screaming for brakes as we ran through Schuyler Street. Here the grade was not so steep, and the speed was diminishing a little; but the canal—I was sure the swinging bridge would be open. I could see it open somewhere behind my eyes, could see us plunging into the black ditch. In my terror, I pulled over the lever, reversed the engine

and gave her steam. The train began to slow and we came to a stop not two feet from the canal. The bridge was closed and the light was green.

It took some time to let off all the brakes. Gander came forward and climbed on the step of the cab.

"What's the matter, kid? Did I scare you? I knew what I was doing and I had them under control every minute."

The blood that had left my icy fingers rushed to my head, and I called that whiskered old goat every one of the Old Man's oaths that I could remember. He laughed indulgently and dropped back onto the rails.

No one, not a shack or Gander or Jim Fancy, ever mentioned that mad run; but sometimes Gander, when he saw me at a distance, went through the motions of blowing a whistle and wiping his eyes.

As for Jim Fancy, after that night he treated me with good-natured indifference, but he didn't "mister" me again. The next time the ghost walked, he wasted no time hanging around the enginehouse with the boys. He deadheaded to Clayville, liquored up, got into a fight and bit off a neighbor's nose. The sheriff threw him into jail for ten days, and that finished him with the Old Man.

Every once in a while we got word of Jim. His father died and he lived in the cabin, trapping and fishing and coming into town occasionally for a spree. About three years later he was run over and killed on the railroad tracks not far from his cabin. He was not drunk, they said, but trying to save a buck that had caught its leg in a trestle.

"Joe," said the Old Man when he heard about it, "if God had given me the brains of a monkey, I could have made a man of Jim."

"Yes," I agreed, "like taming a panther or a tiger." But both of us knew that Jim had been found too late.

15. The Hanging of Big Miller

AS WE LAY ON THE SIDING AT WATERVILLE one day, waiting for a local passenger, Bill Tiffany, the conductor of the coal train I was running, called me out of the cab.

"Want to see Plum Lummis?" he asked. "That's him over there, that gray old man with the campaign hat and the swagger."

I walked over beside the freight office and stared at the old man, until the train came in and he drove away in a buggy with high wheels that had once been painted red. It was pulled by a handsome roan mare; there never was a Lummis who didn't like good horseflesh.

Plum Lummis, the man who had been hanged three times! Everybody in the Chenango Valley knew the story of this almost legendary scoundrel. In fact, the very limb that was his gallows decorated the only saloon in Waterville. Bill Tiffany knew all about the Lummises, for he had grown up on a farm at the edge of the swamp not more than a mile from the robber fortress.

Before the Civil War the Loomises had been a prominent local family, farmers with one of the most fertile pieces of land in Madison County. That was before old

Wash (George Washington on the church register) met Rhoda Mallet, the pretty school teacher, churning before her kitchen door. He kissed her and had his face slapped so hard that it was love at first sight. This was the local legend, and I stuck to it; but Tiffany said his father always told him that Wash heard how she beat up the constable with a shovel, when he came to arrest her rascally father (a Revolutionary officer turned counterfeiter) and said, "That is the gal for me."

Whichever version of the courtship is the true one, Wash did get Rhoda, and for thirty years they and their nine children terrorized the Chenango Valley. When Tiffany was a boy, the sons—and the daughters too, for that matter—were passing counterfeit money, stealing cattle and horses, wagons, buggies and silver-mounted harness, and disposing of their loot through an underground organization that reached from Canada to New Orleans.

Bill remembered Rhoda. She was an old woman then, gaunt and commanding, and she never came to her door without a shotgun. He believed the story that she brought up the children to steal something for her every time they went to town, even if it was nothing more valuable than a paring knife.

When Bill knew them, old Wash was dead, and young Wash was the leader of the gang. The road to the Lummis farm passed near the house, and the boy used to hide behind the bushes to watch the Lummises gallop by, the hoofs of their horses pounding on the hard mud. They filled him with terror and reluctant admiration. For the Lummises had been sent away to college, they had manners and a smattering of learning and they were the handsomest, best-dressed, best-mounted men in the valley. When they rode through the swamp—Wash on the matchless brown cow pony that he had brought from Texas, Grove on Flying Cloud, the black stallion for which he had refused six thousand dollars, and Plum on the finest home-bred horse from his neighbor's barns—they were such dashing rascals that they would have been the beaus of the hop-pickers' dances in spite of their reputation. But rather than pay the fifty cents admission, even in counterfeit money, the boys preferred to break in with clubs. Just plain mean and looking for trouble they were; even the girls were thieves and hard riders, with fingers quick on the trigger.

When they heard the beat of hoofs on the road, the farmers put out their lights and hid. If one of them complained that he had been robbed or paid in counterfeit bills for a yoke of oxen, his house was burned, or his barn, or he was winged by a bullet on some dark turn of the road.

"Still, you couldn't help admiring a knave who was clever enough to sell a man his own horse," Bill always said. The farmer might have more than a suspicion that the coal-black mare he lost was the horse which the Lummises wanted to sell him, even if she did have a white star on her forehead. The farmers knew that a man could bleach a white star on a horse's hide by applying a poultice of hot potatoes, if he didn't mind torturing the horse; they knew that white markings could be colored by nitrate of silver; but if they had their suspicions, they paid their money and said nothing.

But there was a man in Waterville who couldn't stomach all of this outlawry, who thought it ridiculous that the wealthiest farmers in the county should be so terrorized that they went on the Lummises' bail whenever the boys got into trouble. Sheriff Filkins was a little man, according to Bill, but he had the courage of a fighting cock. The Lummises shot at him and threw him into jail on false charges, but he finally organized a vigilance committee and went after the gang.

Wash fled to California; Grove, who was yanked over a tree branch until he got a permanent crook in his neck, escaped to Canada; and Plum they hanged three times to a maple tree, until he told the secrets of the gang and disgorged the loot they had on hand. The tale of this triple hanging of Plum is strengthened by his own story that he hardened and expanded his muscles and flapped like a dried leaf; but Bill would have none of it. He said they strung Plum up by his thumbs five times before he would talk. Whichever way it happened, Plum was the only Lummis who stayed in the county, and he still owned a good piece of horseflesh, the only evidence of his former grandeur.

As old Plum trotted away from the station and Bill and I argued hotly about the thumbs-versus-neck issue, I noticed that Willis Freeman, Bill's new flagman, was listening with his eyes popping and his mouth hanging wide open. Bill, following my glance, raised his voice and asked me, "Ever see a man hanged?"

Seeing what he was up to, I shook my head. "Did you?"

"Yes, I did once. Horrible it was, too."

He was off on his favorite story, about the time he and

a couple of his crew went fishing in the Chenango, somewhere below Norwich. Night came suddenly with a rainstorm, and they took shelter in a haybarn close to the river. In the morning, at daybreak, Bill turned over in the straw and opened his eyes to see the body of a man dangling from the rafters. With a shriek, he ran out of the barn, followed by the two shacks; the last one bumped against the body as he made for the door. They ran most of the way to Norwich, knocked up the sheriff who hadn't had his breakfast, and before they deadheaded back to Utica, learned that the corpse was a suicide.

Bill told his story well—how well, I realized as I watched the face of Willis Freeman. When he felt my eyes on him, he flushed to the ears and, turning on his heel, went back to the caboose. Tiffany looked after him.

"Joe, that man's the biggest nut I ever came across. If he knows anything at all, I haven't found it out. He was never meant for a railroad man; he shivers at every toot of the whistle. I think a screech owl must have frightened his mother before he was born. Wish I could scare him some way so he would quit the railroad."

"Take him down to Norwich and show him your corpse," I suggested. "Maybe that will make a man of him."

My careless remark gave Bill Tiffany an idea, which he tried out on me the next day when we took water at the Grecian Bend. How about staging a hanging to scare Willis? The swamp would be the place, and he was pretty sure Big Miller, the fireman, would play the corpse, if we put it to him in the right way. Miller would make a superb corpse. He was a wide, solid six-feet-two, but nervous as a girl. I knew that it would take a lot of assuring to get him to the sticking point.

I popped the idea when he was eating lunch (he was always happiest when he was eating, although he never seemed to get enough). One tray of his double dinner pail was filled with vegetables, the other with thin strips of raw pork, which he held up and ate like spaghetti. On one side of the pail hung a quart of jelly and on the other a small ham—a two-day supply, but it was always gone before the end of the second day, and he was famished by the time we reached Utica. Sometimes he brought along a couple of dozen duck eggs and ate them all at a sitting, except one which he gave me for politeness' sake.

"Lum," I promised, "I'll get Mamie to bake you an apple pie with raisins in it, if you'll be the corpse."

He liked the idea of having the star part, but he was nervous about the arrangements. He wanted to be sure that we had plenty of engine piston packing along, to pad him under the arms; and that Al Haley, the front shack, would cut him down the minute the show was over. Bill and I spent several days organizing the hanging. Brookfield was the obvious place to stage it. We had a forty minute wait-over there for a couple of passenger trains, and if we stole another hour we would have plenty of time.

The siding at Brookfield ran into dense woods—cedars and sycamores tangled with vines and creepers; rotting, fallen trees and old stumps. In wet weather it was a mire, but this was July, and the pools of moldering leaves were dry, packed mud. For a couple of days we explored the place, looking for a tree with a stout branch overhanging a stump on which Lum could stand while waiting for the hanging. We found it at the end of a small natural clearing, not too far away from the track—a perfect little amphitheater, with the gallows directly in the middle of the stage and nothing to obstruct the view.

On the day of the execution, we began to "make up" Lum the minute we left Waterville. Under his shirt Al wrapped a thick wadding of cylinder packing, which was like a soft, two-inch rope. For the gallows rope we used a length of bell cord hooked to the packing and drawn through the neck of Lum's shirt. With soot from the gauge lamp I made deep circles around his eyes, and I stiffened his hair with soap to make it stand on end.

"Now don't forget to open your eyes wide and hang out your tongue," Al reminded him.

All the way from Binghamton we had been making time. Tiffany had fixed the indicator clock in the caboose so there would be no tell-tale record when we hit it up to thirty or forty miles. The indicator was a ribbon of paper that rolled about a little drum turned by the caboose wheels. The pencil that jiggled across it, recording the rate of speed, was run by a clock. There were two methods of putting it out of order, each so simple that a child could think of it. If we squirted water through the keyhole, the paper puckered and retarded the pencil; or if we hit the clock on its bottom side with a hammer, the pencil jumped up and broke the lead. The only other precaution was to ask the operator at Brookfield to put us in an hour late.

This brass-pounder was a lazy, good-humored fellow who liked his nap between trains and had rigged up a clever warning system. He screwed a hook into one of the cross-beams of the roof, ran a heavy cord through it, tied one end to the coal bucket and the other to the rail. When the train cut the cord, the bucket dropped and the clatter brought him up, awake and alert as a pointer about to flush a covey of partridges. We all knew about his alarm but never let him down; so we counted on his help in stealing time.

When we got in, the station was empty. The passengers hadn't begun to gather for Numbers 3 and 16 (the meet for which we had to wait), but we knew that before another half hour they would be collecting on the platform. Tiffany came by the cab with Willis Freeman and called to Al and me (Lum Miller was hidden in the tender): "We're going into the woods to see if the wild strawberries are ripe. Want to come along?"

"Guess not," I called back. "It's too hot."

As soon as they were out of sight, Lum, Al, and I jumped out of the cab and made for the stump in the cedars. Tiffany had promised to give us half an hour in which he would keep Willis out of sight, showing him the landmarks of the Lummis gang, the sites of murders and hangings, filling him with horrors. It took us no time at all to get ready. Al skinned up the tree and tied the rope, and Lum climbed the stump, ready to step off when he heard Willis and Tiffany crashing through the underbrush.

"Don't forget to stick out your tongue," we cautioned a last time. He was a terrifying sight in the half-darkness of the woods, with his hair sticking up and his eyes white and staring in his blackened face. A wild grapevine, strangling a half-dead sycamore behind him, dangled in ugly, swaying knots; and on a leafless branch, a woodpecker with a white spot on its tail beat a mournful tattoo.

When Lum was ready, we hid behind a clump of cedars and listened. Presently we heard Bill Tiffany and Willis coming through the swamp to the left of us, making a lot of noise. We couldn't see them, but we could hear Bill's voice.

"And it was just about here some place that the Lummises hanged old John Sawyer. He got rarin' mad when they stole his daughter, Josie, and did too much talking, saying he was going to lay for them with a shotgun. The boys burnt down his house and brought him into the swamp and strung him up. I was just a kid then, and I used to come through this way to get the cows; but one night, just at dusk, I almost bumped into him hanging from a sycamore tree, and I didn't stop yelling until I got to Waterville."

The voices were coming nearer. "W—was he dead?" Willis's voice quavered.

"Yeah, I guess so, but I didn't stop to see. Let's have a look. I guess it must have been just about here." The footsteps stopped at the far edge of the clearing. Suddenly Willis let out a shriek that almost lifted my scalp. We could hear him running through the thicket, thrashing about like a frightened elephant.

As soon as we were sure he and Bill Tiffany were out of sight, we cut down Lum and made a beeline for the siding. As we tumbled into the cab, we saw Willis loping out of the woods toward the rail fence that separated it from the railroad. He didn't try to climb it but made a flying leap, missed, and landed on his back. With one terrified glance over his shoulder, he got to his feet and jumped again. This time he made it and charged down the track, his face purple, his shirt sticking to his skin, as wet as if he had been in the creek.

"There's a man hanging in the swamp," he yelled, bringing up at the platform, which by this time was crowded with passengers.

Old Palmer, the man who pumped the water for the tank, heard him first. He was crippled with rheumatism, but he managed to get around pretty fast when he was excited. He hobbled after Willis and followed him into the crowd on the platform, shouting, "Where is he, where is he? Don't cut him down until the coroner comes."

Willis was gabbling, "I could smell him, I tell you. He must have been dead for a long time."

Palmer made a masterly gesture, gathering in forty or fifty passengers who were waiting for the trains.

"Come on, show us where he is," he urged, but Willis was shaking so hard that he had to lean against the station wall. He hung back.

"I wouldn't go into that woods again for a thousand dollars. Get Tiffany. He will take you."

Bill had been edging toward the coal train.

"Holy Jehoshaphat," he muttered to Lum and me (by

that time we were out oiling the engine). "I never counted on all this crowd."

"Come on, Tiffany," shouted old Palmer, "show us where he was."

The crowd pushed around him. Lum and I got back on the other side of the engine, and he looked pretty white in spite of the traces of lampblack that a hasty rub had left on his face.

"But I didn't see him," protested Tiffany. "I don't know where he is."

"Then what made you run," Willis demanded.

"Oh, I ran because you did."

Palmer grabbed Willis by the shoulder and pushed him down the track. The men climbed the rails and helped the lame old man. Even the women followed to the fence.

We who were left behind looked at each other in uncomfortable silence. Affairs had taken a turn that we hadn't expected, and our little joke on Willis was getting out of hand. After a while Tiffany said nervously, "I'm going back and get in the caboose."

Number 3 came in and, a few minutes later, Number 16, on the other side. The agent threw on some express and a couple of mail bags, and one or two women got on; but most of them waited for their men. The trains pulled out, and the passengers who got off sniffed the excitement. A nosy little man in shirt sleeves untied a horse from the hitching-rack and went to get the coroner. We had our orders to clear and were debating whether we should go without Willis, when the coroner came rattling up in a cart and hurried over to ask us what the trouble was.

We told him that we hadn't seen anything and couldn't imagine what had frightened Willis. By that time the investigators were straggling out of the woods, with old Palmer doing most of the talking. The sheriff, who had just arrived, fired a lot of questions at Willis; but he was so confused that he couldn't give an intelligible answer. Everybody was convinced that he had been seeing things.

We hurried him into the caboose and steamed out before the passengers waked up to the fact that there wouldn't be another train either way for at least three hours. The most disappointed one of them all was old Palmer. He talked so much about the crime that someone nailed a sign on the fence, "Here is where the man was hanged." It stayed there until it weathered so gray that the letters faded out.

16. No Flies on Grover

SUMMER AND WINTER WE HAULED COAL. The "season" was in the summer, when the canal was open; but I remember best the winter runs with ice on the rails and snow in our faces, or wind so sharp that we came home as bleary-eyed as if we had been on a spree for a month. Every so often a conductor caught pneumonia or an engineer ran into a hind end in the fog, broke his bones and smashed his engine, and the Old Man made new combinations on the call board.

Shorty ran his train over a bank and wrecked his engine. She turned over three times before she hit the bottom. By some miracle of the road, he and Rags got out alive (Rags had a big cut on her back). The Old Man put Shorty to running a pump in the roundhouse, where he stayed, a bitter, humiliated old man. His clothes, once so spotless, got shabbier and shabbier and the musk stronger. For some reason that I never knew, the Old Man hated Shorty and never let him have another chance.

I played in better luck; Old Tom gave me Number 20, a big new "hog," as we called the freight engines. This was the *A. C. Salsbury*, a Dickson Mogul without a touch of brass. The "Sable Prince" I called it, a good engine but a little logy on the upgrade. All winter I ran that engine; she was my favorite of them all, after dainty old Number 1 with the silver dollars in her bell.

One morning in the spring when I brought in a string of gondolas and climbed out of the Sable Prince, I found the Old Man waiting for me.

"Goddamn it, Joe," was his greeting, "why don't you put out your light?" While I climbed up and snuffed out the headlight, he stood glowering at me.

"I'm going to put you in extra passenger service," he said. "Probably I'm crazy, but it's my own responsibility. Somebody's got to get Number 6 on time." Mr. Halstead, the General, Manager, raised hell when this crack mainliner failed to make connections at Binghamton for New York, and I knew that the engineer had been having trouble with the steam and stabbing the New York train. My blood pressure was going up. At last I was on the fast time schedule, and even if I couldn't pull an express train every day, "extra passenger" was full of variety—picnic trains in the summer, carrying the officials on inspection trips, pulling the pay car and occasional chances at a regular passenger.

Mr. Salsbury, the superintendent, usually went out with the pay car, and he was popular with the boys, always a pleasant word for everybody. One day as we were leaving Binghamton on our return trip, he came front and said to me, "We don't have to make any stops on the way home, Joe. I don't want to go into the ditch, but I'd like to get home in time for the ball game."

We pulled out smartly with a clear board, and I let out the engine to fifty, sometimes sixty, on the stretches. It was pretty going, and I sat back comfortably on my cushion, sniffing the ripening apples in the orchards along the track and listening to the wheels beating out a tune on the rail joints. The conductor pulled the whistle on me, and when we swung wide going around the Grecian Bend, I slowed down; but I eased out the throttle again when I figured he had forgotten.

We pulled into the yards at Utica a little after two o'clock. Mr. Salsbury came down the steps of the pay car, dusting off his knees, and I saw that he looked hot and grimy, with his hair mussed up.

"Well, Joe," he said. "I've arrived in time for the game, and we didn't go into the ditch; but you tipped over the coin box and spilled twenty-four thousand dollars on the floor. We've been on our knees ever since we left Oxford!"

During the summer and fall of '92, when Grover Cleveland and General Benjamin Harrison were fighting a lively presidential campaign, we ran specials every day or two. In upper New York state, politics was a serious sport. Our section was strongly for Cleveland, and each town had its Cleveland-and-Stevenson club, which paraded through the home streets on every possible occasion and frequently chartered a train to visit a neighboring town for a monster celebration.

In Utica the Cleveland boys called themselves the "Jacksonians" and dressed up in high hats and gaudy oilcloth uniforms in the style of the 1840's—expensive but none too stout red, white and blue products of a local costumer. On the evening that the Jacksonians went to Waterville, at least two hundred turned out. I was assigned to pull the special train. When we backed the coaches into the station at seven o'clock, we could hear the band playing *There'll Be a Hot Time in the Old Town Tonight*, and, above the noise of the brasses, the cheering of the crowd, the popping of firecrackers and the *clump, clump* of marching feet.

Soon a crowd of small boys and dogs, forerunners of the parade, charged down Genesee Street and behind them came the brass band of thirty pieces, splitting the air, with the August sun glittering on their shining buttons and wide gold stripes. Behind them marched five Jacksonians with a banner made of four panels about six feet square, joined together like the four sides of a box. One man carried the pole on which it was mounted, and the other four held it steady with guy ropes strung from the corners.

In one panel was a portrait of Grover Cleveland. This was carried facing front, and opposite him, facing the Jacksonians, was Adam Stevenson. On the sides were big-muscled, contented-looking workmen smoking cigars. In their pockets were more cigars—great, fat Pittsburgh stogies. Dinner pails swung from their hands, and from the pails dangled several fat chickens. Everybody was going to eat chicken if the Democrats won.

Behind the banner marched the Jacksonians with kerosene torches in their hands, making a roof of thick, pungent smoke. The costumes made the fat men seem fatter, the tall men, lanker, and the short ones more runty than usual; but everyone was gay and pranced to the music, while the children yelled and the dogs barked.

The police cleared a space on the platform, and the Jacksonians lined up for a farewell drill. The boys in the band took a deep breath and began *Tramp, Tramp, Tramp, the Boys Are Marching*, while the Jacksonians right-about-faced, marched eight steps back, side-stepped to right and left and ended with a couple of brothers off the edge of the platform and a half dozen of them pointed the wrong direction. When they were straightened out again, the drum major raised his baton and led their war cry. With a mighty roar they shouted,

> *Rah, rah, rah,*
> *There are no flies on Grover!*
> *There are no flies on Grover!*
> *There may be one or two on Ben*
> *But there are no flies on Grover.*
> *Rah, rah, rah.* CLEVELAND! STEVENSON!

By the time they reached "Stevenson," the Jacksonians were so purple in the face and out of breath that they garbled it. The name was never designed for a war cry, and the only distinguishable syllable was the "-son."

As the Jacksonians broke ranks and piled into the coaches, Dan, my fireman, looked back and said that they couldn't possibly squeeze in; but somehow they managed it, all except the banner committee, who couldn't get the banner through the doors. They came to the engine, dragging Cleveland and Stevenson tilted at an undignified angle, and asked Dan what could be done about it. For a couple of bucks they persuaded him to take care of it. He could put the staff in the coal, and it looked safe enough, with the guy ropes tied to the tank.

We got the highball and were on our way. Waterville was no more than an hour's run, but the train was too heavy for such a small engine, and it was going to take good work to get us up the grade. Danny kept the steam up, and the sparks shot merrily out of the diamond stack. As we were going through Sauquoit, almost at the top of the hill, he gave a scream.

"Joe, Joe, Cleveland's afire." I looked back and saw the banner flaming. Already Cleveland and Stevenson were blackened ashes, and the fire was licking around the stogies and the chickens in the workmen's dinner pails. In a minute there was nothing left of the sweet dream of prosperity but the staff. Danny had a face as long as Paris Hill.

"What the devil can I tell them when we get to Waterville?" I didn't know, but I felt sorry for the kid and said I'd think of something.

"Make yourself scarce when we pull in. I'll hand out some line to them. But, whatever you do," I urged him, "hang onto your two bucks. They'll have to parade the minute they get off the train, and after the party is over, they won't be in a condition to start anything."

As we eased up to the Waterville station, Danny jumped to the ties and disappeared behind the freight shed. While the Jacksonians piled out onto the platform, where the local Jacksonians were lined up to greet them, the committee came to the engine for the banner. I leaned out and told them the sad news, adding that Danny burnt his hands trying to put out the fire and blistered them so badly that I sent him to find a doctor. They were annoyed, especially the man who carried the staff; but the

band had already struck up a march, so he gave a tug to his white cotton gloves and thanked me for Danny's efforts. There was nothing left for the committee to do but to fall in at the end of the parade.

While we were loafing around, waiting for the Jacksonians to finish their celebrating, Andy Ferguson, the conductor, came front and sat in the cab. This was the first time he and I had been on a run together since he had left Dad Burr's freight, when he was promoted to conductor of a coal train.

"Want to see the fist of God Almighty?" he asked me. Drawing out of his pocket a slip of paper, the front half of an envelope that had been neatly slit around the edges, he handed it to me. On the back of it was written, in the thin, spidery hand of the president of the road: "Pass Mr. Josiah Stearns from New York to Utica."

"We get some passes from old Halstead and a lot from the Supe, of course, but this is the first one I've seen from Sloane, and I thought I'd keep it," Andy said. "They say he could give the devil points on how to make a fellow rattle in his shoes."

Andy folded the pass and stuck it carefully in his pocket. In those days not even the president of a railroad had memorandum pads with his name printed at the top. It was the custom to use the backs of envelopes for all sorts of memoranda, and passes were usually in the form of these hand-written envelope notes, even when they were good for a year. If the conductor was in a good humor and liked the holder of a one-trip pass, he didn't take it up; and the holder used it again and again, as long as his luck held good.

Andy and I gossiped about Sheep-face and old Sitting Bull until the Jacksonians began to stagger back to the train. Danny had stayed in the tender, but he saw that now he was perfectly safe: they couldn't have told him from a telegraph pole. They looked like the straggling end of Washington's army after it had crossed the Delaware. No one was shouting "There are no flies on Grover!" or yodeling for Stevenson. Some were being led, others carried, and still others weaved along under their own power, mightily pleased with themselves. Even the members of the band carried their trumpets upside down and slung over their shoulders or dragging on the ground.

Danny went boldly onto the platform and helped to shift them into the coaches.

"Ding-dong," shouted the drum major, trying to lean on his baton, but his legs were made of rubber. Andy pushed him into the vestibule and shut the door. He gave us the highball, Danny leaped to the step of the cab and fell onto his seat, while I took up the slack.

"I gotta watch the fire," he shouted. "It's going to be harder than dragging coal to get this bunch of souses over Paris Hill."

Pulling an overload of tipsy Jacksonians was hazardous, but the most spine-chilling ride of them all was the run I made to Richfield Springs with Old Tom in the cab. It happened to be one of the few times that any of us ever saw the Old Man make a fumble, but he twisted it so neatly that he left me catching my breath in indignant admiration.

As I came out of the roundhouse one afternoon, ready to go home, Tom stood in the doorway of his office and shouted to me. He ordered me to take an engine to Richfield Springs right away. The one that was hauling a picnic train had broken down, and the Old Man was harrowed with a vision of the Methodist Sunday School from Chenango Forks running wild at the Springs—crying babies, indignant mothers, even the elders getting belligerent on too many beers. As I turned back across the yard, he grabbed his cap and came after me.

"I'll go along and be conductor."

Number 10 was a sweet new engine with every latest gadget, high wheels for speed and not an extra ounce of weight. When the Old Man climbed on, he looked her over lovingly and said, "I'll run her, Joe." I slipped off the runner's seat and went over to stand on the fireman's side, where I could keep my eye on the board. I wondered how long it had been since he had touched a throttle. He was cautious enough going over the drawbridge and out Schuyler Street, but when he got over the crossing where one-legged Herman Crouse flagged us ahead, he let her out and she shot up the grade like a jack rabbit.

"We've got to stop at New Hartford," I reminded him, "and hole up for Number 3."

Reluctantly he backed into the siding and waited for the passenger to unload. Andy Ferguson, who had been ordered to meet us there, dropped off and came over to the siding. When he saw the Old Man at the throttle, he gave me a startled look, but neither of us said a word as we stood together on the front end of the tender.

We got to the Junction in fine style, switched onto the branch track and began to climb the hill toward the Springs, shooting around the lakes, roaring into the depressions and out again with the throttle wide open and the stack shooting sparks like a Roman candle. The fireman, a youngster, stoked like mad, with one nervous eye on the Old Man, the other on the indicator; and every once in a while I poked out a clinker for him, raked the coal to the corners or gave him a warning look when he was about to smother his fire with over-zeal (remembering my own first trip and the sullen core that refused to glow). He needn't have worried, for Old Tom paid not the slightest heed to any of us. He was hanging out the window feeling the wind of our motion in his whiskers, tooting at the startled cows and shrieking over the crossings.

The engine held fairly well to the track on the upgrade, but when we dropped into Cedarville swamp, we hit one of the roughest stretches on the line, and she shimmied like an Egyptian dancer at a fair. Old Tom did not slow down. Andy cocked his head at me, but there was nothing either of us could do except pray and keep our eyes on the rails ahead. At the same instant we saw a telegraph pole half uprooted, leaning over the track.

"Stop her! Pull her over and goose her!" I yelled, begging Tom to put her in reverse and give her the steam. My voice startled him, for he leaned toward the front glass and stared ahead, but he didn't understand what I had said or see the pole until it was too late. Andy and I ducked behind the boiler and pulled down the fireman. Above the screeching protest of the wheels under Tom's delayed brake, we heard a ripping and tearing as if the whole top of the engine was being sheared away.

When the cab stopped quivering, we picked ourselves

up and looked around. Miraculously, the front window was not smashed in. Old Tom was already on the ties looking at the damage. The pole had sliced off the headlight, the stack and the bell before the engine pulled it free and tossed it into the field. The splintered glass was lying along the ties, and the twisted metal of the stack. The bell, the pride of Number 10's regular engineer, gleamed in a brackish little puddle full of leaves. Old Tom went back and pushed it over with his toe, looking at the hollow punched in the side. His beard waggled piteously as he climbed on the running board and squinted down the hole where the stack had been. His proud new engine, the best on the line, was a headless trunk. When he raised his face, I could have sworn I saw a tear in his good eye.

"Get in, Joe," he ordered, "and see if she'll start."

I hoisted myself up the handrail, released the brake, gave her a whisper of steam and felt her begin to roll; there was nothing the matter with the engine. Tom and Andy and the dazed fireman climbed on, but the Old Man motioned me to keep at the throttle. We were only ten miles from the Springs, and we crept along, trying to see through the cloud of smoke and cinders that belched from the hole directly in front of the glass. I told the boy not to fire as long as we had an ounce of steam. Andy got down on the step and hung out as far as he could, peering under the smoke.

For a mile or two, the Old Man was silent. Out of the corner of my eye I watched him hissing through his teeth, as if he were talking to himself. As we were limping into South Columbia, the station nearest to the Springs, I thought we might as well have a little fun. There was no sense in acting as if we were going to a funeral. After I tooted through the station, I looked around and grinned at the Old Man.

"Whew," I said to him, "I'd hate to go before Mr. Thatcher after this."

"Joe, you know I didn't see it."

Andy and the fireman smiled uneasily at the humility in his voice.

"Yes, but that won't go with him. You can't put that over on Mr. Thatcher."

Old Tom stiffened and looked as if he were going to ram me with his beard.

"Tell you what, Joe. I can fix the other engine; nothing's wrong with it but the brake. I'll take the picnic train back with it. You get a barrel and stick it on in front here for a stack. You can get her in that way. And don't say anything about it in the shop. They'll think you did it. You're perfectly capable of it!" He spat the last words at me, and this time the Old Man grinned.

Andy waggled his fingers from his perch on the step behind Tom's back, and the fireman covered his face with his bandanna to smother a giggle. It was practically impossible to get ahead of the Old Man.

17. Engine 26

B Y THE SPRING OF '92, THE LACKAWANNA
was running two milk trains a day on
the Utica Division, one from Utica, the
other from Richfield Springs—big, heavy trains of twelve
or fifteen cars, the fastest on the road. The one from the
Springs was a nighthawk, connecting at Binghamton with
a mainliner that got the milk to New York in the morning. There were only one or two engines on the Division
heavy enough to pull them; so Scranton ordered a new
engine, and the Old Man built it in the Utica shops.

For months the boys talked about her in the enginehouse: her size (she was going to be one of the heaviest
that rolled); her two cabs, one for the engineer, one for
the fireman; the gold leaf and the brass and the fine woods
that were going into her cabs. Evidently the Old Man was
shooting the works.

Fred Willkie, his ace engineer, was to run her; and
what the Old Man didn't think of in the way of trimmings, Fred bought out of his own pocket. When Number 26 finally steamed into the enginehouse, we hung
around her stall, exclaiming at her style and congratulating
Fred. She *was* a beauty: a large cylinder Mother Hubbard

with small wheels, a powerful boiler, and every gadget known to the Old Man. The front cab was made of black walnut, with bird's-eye maple panels. Fred was so proud of it that he waxed the wood inside and out, and he spent money like a yokel at a fair—fifteen dollars to the Williams headlight factory for painting the American flag on each side of the headlight, and heaven knows how much for gold leaf and brass.

The Old Man told Fred to take two or three days to break her in; and he and the superintendent both went along on the first trip to the Junction, all of them excited as children going to a picnic. I was in the yard when they pulled out, and I have never seen a prouder man than Willkie, as he hung out the window of 26 and slid her out of the yard. The Old Man was standing behind him, whiskers waggling as he listened to the shortening swoosh of the exhaust when she picked up speed.

The next day Fred took her to Binghamton, with orders to meet a coal train at Brisben; but he was so interested in her performance that he forgot everything else. Running through Brisben, he smashed into the coal train and piled up on the bank. Luckily he was not making speed, so no one was killed; but Number 26 was pretty well wrecked.

I was following behind with the morning passenger and heard about the smash-up from the operator at Brisben. He was a good friend of Fred's and looked as if he were going to a wake.

"Fred'll get bounced," he said. "He hasn't got a rabbit's chance." A brakeman had come running back to stop the traffic and send for the wrecking master to clear the track. In about fifteen minutes Fred and his fireman came along the ties, Fred hanging his head as if he never wanted to see a living soul. They cleaned up their faces, covered with dust and cinders from the ballast. There was not enough damage to worry about, but you could slice the gloom over all of them with a knife. I kept out of the way, for it is an unhappy thing to see another man's misfortune.

The agent was right about Willkie; he was taken off the service. But he was such a fine engineer (one of the best on the division) and so well liked by the Brotherhood, that they put up a strong argument to the superintendent. Maybe it wasn't so difficult to persuade him, for he knew how Willkie loved that engine. When she had her cab patched up at the repair shop, she came back looking almost as good as new. Old Tom gave her to Willkie again and put them on the Richfield Springs run, making the trip every other day, with a day at home between runs. I was taken off "extra passenger" and given the alternate run; and I strutted like a turkey gobbler, for this was my first chance on a regular schedule.

The Old Man called us into the office and told us that, as we knew, the enginehouse at the Springs had only two stalls and no facilities for repair. He gave us authority to hire a watchman, and added that the longer the engine ran without needing to come into the Utica shops for repair, the less time we would lose, laid off and waiting. That was like him: practically ordering us to make our own repairs, but never giving us an extra screwdriver or monkey wrench.

Fred liked the idea of being on our own, so he suggested that we lift two or three driving springs and other spare equipment and bury them under the coal. Driving springs were always breaking, and it was a lot of work to replace them; but we could manage with local help.

For some time the engine ran as sweetly as you please. Number 26 left the Springs at nine o'clock in the evening and had the highball all the way, except at Chenango Forks, where we took on ice. By two in the morning we were in Binghamton, and by eleven the milk was in Hoboken, ready for delivery in New York. There was a thrill about that ride, shooting through dark little towns alone in the cab, the engine and I the only creatures awake. The headlights swung on the double curves, picking up the rails first on one side, then on the other; and in the swamp the whistle echoed three or four times, bouncing from the hills.

The enginehouse at the Springs we considered our own private property. We were the only regular crew that used it. The passenger engines as a rule went back to the Junction or to Utica. An occasional coal engine spent the night in the second stall; but for the most part we had the place to ourselves.

We found an accommodating old Englishman named Erbert for watchman. (No doubt his name had originally been "Herbert," but nobody called him that.) He wasn't very clean, but he wiped the engine well enough and was always fixing up little comforts, like the shower bath that he made for us by putting a big tin of water in the cupola of a caboose, attaching a hose to it and fastening a perforated tin can onto the end of the hose. He didn't mind lugging water to the improvised tank, but he was not so eager to sweep or wash down the engine.

Erbert wouldn't be much help for repairs, we could see; but Fred was resourceful. One morning he told me that he had found a prize, a blacksmith named Hennessey, who lived at Bridgewater, about fifteen miles up the line. The man was moving his shop to the Springs and bringing his family later. He had proposed to Fred that, if we let him commute on the engine, he would do any small welding or repair jobs that we needed.

It was a perfect arrangement for us, giving us practically a shop of our own; but the blacksmith's first enthusiasm wore off after a few weeks, when Fred had stuck him for several new wrenches, packing irons, and gadgets that must have taken a lot of time. We were getting decidedly the best of the arrangement. Then, on one of my days off in Utica, the caller pounded on my door and said that Mr. Thatcher and Mr. Salsbury, the superintendent, wanted to see me over in the office. Mamie looked worried; but no matter what scrape I was in, she was ready to fight for me. She was giving me a late breakfast in the kitchen, with eggs from her own hens and bacon spitting on the skillet.

"Drink your coffee," she said. "It won't hurt them to wait a minute." I swallowed the coffee and cut across to the yard, eating one of her hot buttered biscuits on the way. Outside the office I brushed off the crumbs and set my face for whatever the Old Man was going to hand out.

Tom cut loose as soon as he saw me standing in front of the bar.

"Joe," he shouted, being extra tough in front of the superintendent, "by whose authority did you hire a blacksmith to make company repairs and run up a bill for a hundred and fifty dollars? A hundred and fifty dollars, mind you—a hundred and fifty dollars!" The indignation in his voice was so profound that oaths would have been superfluous.

I caught my breath. Here was the time to think quickly and keep from involving Willkie, but my tongue wouldn't limber up. Mr. Salsbury, a quiet man, gave me a reassuring glance.

"Tom," he suggested, "I notice that only one item is charged to Joe. The rest seems to be authorized by Willkie."

"Don't you fool yourself, Albert. No matter who had the work done, this is the man who framed the whole damned business." He shoved at me a bill that he had been waving under my nose. I saw that it was a statement in Hennessey's heavy, painstaking lettering, itemizing all the tools he had made for us and the repair work he had done on the engine. At the bottom in fat, black figures was the even total, one hundred and fifty dollars.

"It's yours," threatened the Old Man. "Take it, and if it is not paid within twenty-four hours, you and Willkie will both be suspended from the service until you can show me a receipt."

I caught the next train for Richfield Springs and all the

way kept trying to think of some scheme for cancelling the bill. Raising the money was not even worth considering; it would have been as easy for us to kidnap the King of England and deliver him to Old Tom in a bathing suit as it would be to raise a hundred and fifty dollars in twenty-four hours.

It was five o'clock when I got to the Springs; we had three hours and a little over in which to save our skins. Fred was in the enginehouse showing Erbert how to paint the stack; but when he saw my face, he ran toward me, asking, "What's the funeral?" When he heard my news, his first reaction was to punch Hennessey in the nose; but I had already discarded that idea. The blacksmith could lick us both at the same time, with one hand tied behind his back.

"Let's go over to his house," I suggested—by this time he had moved to Richfield Springs—"and try the sympathy act. You were always good at handing out a sob story. You could tell him about our wives and starving children, while I sit by with a sad look on my face." Willkie was unmarried, and Mamie would have scorned the idea that she needed protection; but Willkie was never hampered by facts.

Fred could think of no better plan, so we asked Erbert, who knew everything, where Hennessey lived. He concluded his directions with the remark that Hennessey always got sentimental with a couple of beers, so we picked up three bottles on the way and went to call on the man.

He was not in the shop but we found him behind the cottage, digging in a little back garden.

"Good," whispered Willkie. "Planting puts you in a gentle mood, you know—flowers and radishes and things." I remembered Mamie's ferocity about rose beetles, but hoped he was right; for the muscles of Hennessey's shoulders bulged under the thin shirt, from which he had torn the sleeves, and I wouldn't have wanted to tangle with those brawny, ape-like arms covered with long, black fuzz.

"What you planting, Hennessey?" called Fred as we went over and sat on the back step, without waiting for an invitation.

"Tomatoes," answered Hennessey, looking at us a bit sheepishly. He knows he overcharged us, I thought; but if we don't handle him right, he'll get his Irish up and be truculent about it.

"Come on over and rest a minute," Fred said, taking the bottles of beer from the paper sack under his arm. Solemnly he pulled off the caps with his teeth and handed them to us. When Hennessey saw the foam spilling over, he dropped his hoe and came to sit on the step.

Fred didn't say a word while we took a long swig, and I followed his lead. A spotted hound came out of the kitchen and licked my fingers.

"Nice day," said Fred. We all took another drink. He patted the hound. "Joe has a dog for his kid, the youngest one with the broken leg. Four kids he has, three of 'em girls, and the oldest five years old. I don't know what's going to happen to them now. My oldest's ten, and he'll soon be able to take care of himself; but his mother, she has a graveyard cough, and the baby's only six weeks old. I don't know what they're going to eat, with their dad out of work."

"What happened, Fred?" asked Hennessey uneasily. "You and Joe ain't done nothing to get the sack." He finished his bottle with a mighty gulp, and I quietly handed him mine, which was still half full.

"You don't know the Old Man. He's a fiend," sighed Fred. This, he judged, was the moment to pull out the bill so he spread it on the step between him and Hennessey. "You wouldn't think he'd be so unreasonable about this, but he's a raging furnace. He vows he'll bounce us if we don't get it receipted within twenty-four hours; and he'll blacklist us with every road in the country. Can't even get on a construction gang. It's digging ditches for Joe and me, I guess. I wouldn't mind so much, if it wasn't for the kids. Buddy won't ever get a chance to be an engineer like his dad. The Old Man'll see to that."

I pulled out my handkerchief and dabbed my eyes. It wasn't all bluff: Fred was so mournful and the beer so mellowing that the tears were actually oozing from my eyes. The hound looked up and stuck his cold nose on my cheek. With my free hand I rubbed his ears.

"You know we'd pay you, if we had a cent," I ventured, "even if we did think we were doing you a good turn by carrying you on the engine. But honest, Hennessey, you know we haven't either of us enough money to line a hummingbird's nest. You know how it is, with four children and the youngest under five."

Hennessey finished my bottle and threw it to the other end of the garden, then wiped his hands on the front of his shirt.

"You boys know I didn't mean you any harm. I just thought I could use a little of the railroad's money." He ran up the steps, went into the house, came back with a worn leather wallet in his hand and pulled out of it two five-dollar bills.

"Here, boys, take these. You need them more than I do. My kids are grown." The tears were making tracks down his cheeks and mingling with the suds on his black mustache.

"Mr. Hennessey, you're the grandest man I ever knew," said Fred, with a break in his voice. "We won't take the money, but if you'll just receipt the bill, the Old Man can't fire us, and we'll be able to get along."

Hennessey carried the bill into the house and returned, waving it to dry the ink of his signature, which wandered clear across the page.

"There, I guess that will do you. See, it says 'paid in full.'"

Fred stuck it carefully in his pocket, we all shook hands, I rubbed the hound's ear again and we invited Hennessey to come over to the enginehouse for a glass of beer whenever he felt like it. We turned and waved to him from the end of the street. It was hard not to run or burst out shouting until we were out of sight.

When we got back, old Erbert was making the gesture of sweeping off the deck of Number 26. We grabbed his shoulders and danced him around until his rheumatic bones cracked.

"It's all due to you, Erbert," we shouted. "You and the beer." He looked at the receipted bill and shook his head.

"Hennessey's a pretty tough proposition unless you hit him just right. He broke a man's back last year with his bare hands. I didn't think you could do it."

We went back to the engine. It was time to take out Number 26.

"Fred," I said, "it will be a proud moment for you when you hand this payment in full to the Old Man in the morning. I'd like to see his face." But Fred assured me that he had enjoyed too many proud moments with the Old Man. It was my turn to have the pleasure.

Deadheading back to Utica, I caught a few hours sleep, after I had told Mamie about the four pitiful little children, all under five years.

"You men are easy marks," she said, laughing, as she poured me another cup of coffee. "You'd never catch a woman on a story like that. I bet you a corona the Old Man won't believe you."

But I didn't intend to give Old Tom the satisfaction of scoffing at the tale. In the morning I went over as soon as the office was open, leaned on the rail and laid the bill on the table without saying a word. "Paid in full, J. C. Hennessey," was so black and bold, you could see it clear across the room. Rogers looked at it, cocked his eyebrow inquiringly at me and passed it to Tom, who was sitting behind him at the roll-top desk. Tom gave it one glance and came to the rail, his good eye burning with curiosity.

"How did you make out?" he asked.

"Oh, Willkie and I talked it over. It was such a trifle that we decided to pay it, rather than have any trouble."

"The hell you did. Do you think I'd believe any God-damned lie like that. You couldn't raise it between you to save you from the judgment day." But I smiled and wouldn't say a word.

When he saw that he wasn't going to get anything out of me, he shot out a string of oaths and told me what to

expect if we ever ran up another bill against the Lackawanna. I backed out and went over to the roundhouse,
where the boys were waiting to hear the news. For a long
time they hammered their fists when they passed Willkie
or me, or beat a tattoo on any handy piece of metal, just
to remind us of our blacksmith's bill.

18. The Milk-white Cockerel

THE FIRST TIME WE HAD TO PUT A NEW driving spring in Number 26, Erbert Tilbury advanced a helpful idea. It would take hard muscle-work to replace the spring. We had to jack up the engine on the old screw jacks, and 26 was the heaviest thing on wheels. Erbert suggested that the village boys would work like hunkies for us, if we would permit them to use the enginehouse for their cocking mains.

"Why, Erbert," Fred exclaimed in mock disapproval, "aren't you afraid the constable will get us? You aren't by any chance a fancier?"

Erbert raised one drooping eyebrow and opened his mouth in such a wide smile that tobacco coursed down the two brown gulleys at the corners.

"Aw, I can tell a Dorking from a Gillman Grey."

All the boys owned a cock or two, he told us, and we could get more man-power than we needed, if we were cooperative about the enginehouse for their private mains. These, he said, were small, secret affairs to try out their cocks, nothing to arouse the constable.

There we were with Number 26 waiting for a new

spring; it was a three- or four-hour job, and she had to get out at nine o'clock. So we took a chance, hoping that the Old Man would never get wind of it.

Erbert went into the village and came back with half-a-dozen husky country boys, who had the engine on the jacks in no time. Fred and I crawled under and lay on our backs, taking down the old spring and putting in the new. When we came out, an hour or so later, our faces plastered with oil and grease and our eyes almost blinded with the drippings, Erbert told us to go over to the caboose. He had the shower bath working, and the water had been warming in the sun.

The boys were so fascinated with the engine that we had a hard job to keep them off of it. With the slightest encouragement they would have done all of Erbert's work and the fireman's too. But Fred was so particular that he wouldn't let anyone else touch her; he even liked to polish the brass with his own hands.

On evenings when there was no engine in the other stall, we ran Number 26 out on a switch and thus cleared the enginehouse floor. The boys built a more or less circular pit with planks knocked together, and brought in several bucketfuls of dirt to use on the floor instead of tanbark. One of them made a chalk mark in the approximate center of the pit, with two others about a foot from the center mark, and directly opposite each other, on which to set the cocks.

Generally these meets were held on evenings when I was at the enginehouse to take out the milk, for although Fred approved of the scheme as a means of getting the work done, he was not interested in the cocks. Every minute that wasn't spent in prettying up Number 26, he spent by the lake or in the fields, sketching. He was a talented artist; his drawings were on the walls of the enginehouses in Binghamton and Utica, and the men were always begging him for portraits of their babies or sketches of a hillside or a farmhouse that they wanted to remember. Whenever he was in Utica he hung around the paint shop, salvaging pail ends, from which he mixed a remarkable range of colors.

Once I saw him watching a painter lettering Delaware, Lackawanna & Western on a cab. "Why don't you put just 'Lackawanna'?" he said. "It would look so much better." He took the chalk from the painter's hand and drew "Lackawanna" in high Gothic letters, a precisely spaced, well-proportioned design. The painter filled it in with gold, but the Old Man had a fit. (Not many years later, the name was shortened to "Lackawanna" on all the engines.)

Years after this, Fred had an opportunity to take a few art lessons, and not long ago I saw one of his hillsides in the New York office of one of the officials of the road.

At the Springs, as I mentioned, Fred spent his off time sketching and left me to keep an eye on the meets, with the understanding that they were to be kept very small, and by invitation only—three or four boys with cocks and perhaps a dozen of their friends, "squeezers" who bet a nickel or two on the defeat of a certain bird, and "boosters" who risked their money on his victory. More often the birds were "stags," under a year old, and their owners had no intention of fighting them to the death; but even without steel spurs they sometimes killed each other before they could be uncoupled.

Many a warm night we sat on our heels around the pit. I liked it best when Erbert refereed. The lanterns hanging from the roof beams, lighted up his shrivelled face, his working jaws, and unblinking eyes. The flurry of two birds rising to strike; the tense stillness of the men hunched forward, watching for the spurt of blood from the neck, or the gouged eye—I remember these particularly; and the odors—odors of sweating bodies and chickens and warm blood, and faint above it all, the persistent sweetness of wild honeysuckle from the field next door.

Erbert fought red cocks as a rule, shawl-necks with white legs and black breasts. He bred them himself in two or three runs behind his shack. He mated uncle to niece and aunt to nephew, but never brother to sister or parent to child. Why, he didn't know, but it wasn't done in England and just didn't work that way. Reds, he thought, were better fighters than blacks; but he was always ready to tell us about Bone Crusher, the black that he fought for three years before he retired the bird, a champion even after it was blinded in both eyes. Bone Crusher was a "wheeler"—that is, at first he acted as if he were running away, but when he heard the ringside cries of "dunghill," "wring his neck," and so forth, he wheeled and lighted on his opponent with such terrific speed that he crushed a wing or a leg before the fight had even begun.

And Erbert knew every trick of the pit. He was a fair sportsman, and scorned to push or hold his cocks. When he set his cock beak-to-beak with another, both of them too nearly dead to hold up their heads, he never gained a point by giving his bird a surreptitious boost of the tail, making him appear to peck; but he knew to a nicety the second to pull a couple of feathers just behind the comb, jerking them out with a smart twitch to make the bird peck of his own accord. If his cock was blinded, he never set the bird with the good eye facing the opponent but on a right angle, to allow for the bird's wheeling toward the blind side.

"You've got to have a good fighter," he used to tell the boys, "but half the trick is in the handling." They listened with reverence, eager for tips, and were always hanging around the enginehouse, bringing in birds to learn what Erbert thought of them.

I began to be nervous about it—so many boys with birds in their arms came and went across the yard that I was afraid the constable would get onto it, then the Old Man would hear about it, and there would be the devil to pay. Fred promised to speak to Erbert, but he didn't have the heart to be stern with the old fellow, and Erbert knew it. He was a little more careful and did his judging behind the enginehouse; but almost any afternoon when he should have been wiping the rods of Number 26, you could hear him blasting some lad's hopes.

"Sonny, I thought you said this bird had breeding. Look at his heels. They're huge, and the bone is as big as a walnut. His back's too long, and he's too high off the ground."

"But he's got a grand reach," the boy might say.

"Reach! Reach! What good is a reach, if he hasn't the muscle? Here, pass your thumb over his back. Do you feel any muscle? No, I thought not. And look at his breast bone sticking out like the prow of a boat."

As the summer waned, and Erbert became more and more involved in the local mains, we got very little work out of him. In the big meets the villages competed with each other, thirty or forty cocks on a side; and the betting was often as high as a dollar. Erbert had a half-dozen reds and two or three grays, with which he picked up a bit of extra money; but he was getting off early so many nights that Fred's patience was almost exhausted. The breaking point came when Erbert carelessly thrust a slash bar through the side of Number 26's headlight, smashing one of the American flags, for which Fred had spent his own silver. Erbert was inconsolable. It would cost ten dollars to get a new flag painted, and the old fellow could come by ten dollars about as easily as he could make gold out of coal dust.

"Mr. Willkie," he promised, "if you won't bounce me this time, I'll have the money for you in a month. I swear it."

Fred was still angry, and he put no faith whatever in the old boy's promises. "How are you going to get ten dollars?"

"I can't tell you, but honest I will," he pleaded. Later he whispered to me, "I've got a cock I've been saving that's better than old Bone Crusher. He's the gamest bird you ever saw, milk-white with yellow legs and bill. His neck curves like a racehorse, his eyes are so bold that they almost pop out at you, and his nails are so sharp that he could fight without spurs. I know what I'm talking about. There ain't a cock this side of the Atlantic can touch him."

"Yeah," I said. "He'll probably be blinked in the first main, and then where's your money?"

"Listen," pleaded Erbert. "I got ideas." He wasn't risking the milk-white cockerel on a single meet but wanted to pit him in a Battle Royal, a free-for-all, with the winner taking the entry fees.

I advised him not to tell Fred, who was pretty well fed up with it all and would be sure to think that we would get no work out of him for the rest of the summer. Erbert was a good promoter, and before long he told me that he had five villages in on the scheme, with the fight open to anybody who had a cock and an entry fee of fifty cents. Admission also was to be a half-dollar, and the gate ought to pay for the rent of the barn which Erbert had hired. This barn was a big new one and had cost the farmer three thousand dollars, so he was glad to make a little something on it. Not a word about the milk-white cockerel, he warned us. Anybody who saw him would know that it was a waste of money to enter another bird.

In spite of myself I got interested and spent the next month promoting the fight. Every Lackawanna man on the Utica Division began to hoard a little betting money. One or two of the high-toned passenger engineers who lived in Binghamton were even planning to spend the night in one of the boardinghouses at the Springs. Erbert set the date for a Saturday night, to catch as many of the railroad men as possible.

A week before the match, I found Erbert nailing up a pen of chicken wire and boards behind the engine house when he should have been sweeping.

"Sh-h," he whispered as he put in the last nail. From behind the coop he lifted a basket and, opening it, brought out a white cock with vivid yellow beak and legs. He was about five pounds, I guessed; and as he stretched and arched his neck, erecting his bright red comb, he was so magnificent that I readily believed he could subdue every other bird in the meet. He was tame enough with Erbert and laid his head confidently over the man's elbow, eyeing me with enormous, scornful black eyes.

"Gotta begin feeding him up today."

I went in and looked at the rods of Number 26 to see if Erbert had wiped off the grease, and found them clean as a whistle. He's starting well, anyway, I thought; for I remembered that cocks needed the care of primadonnas for the seven days of conditioning.

"Come see him eat," Erbert said, when he had thrashed a handful of barley in a bag. "This grain's old and thin-shelled and as dry as Hennessey's throat. Tonight His Nibs gets his bread crumbs and port. He's going to live like an earl."

I went out back and watched him scatter the grain in the pen. The bird fell upon it greedily, snapping it up with short jabs, going over the ground with the speed and precision of a mowing-machine.

"Just look at him," gloated Erbert. "Look how red he is in the face. You can always tell a good bird by the way he feeds. If he's finicky and turns black in the face when he exercises, he's no account. You might just as well try to fight a Plymouth Rock."

Late in the afternoon, when I was working on the steam gauge, I heard voices behind the enginehouse and went over to the door to see what was going on. Erbert was sitting on an upturned box with the white cock between his knees, and one of the boys was standing by, holding a red bird. He was showing Erbert the bird's spurs, bandaged with pieces of rag. Erbert was wrapping the spurs of the white warrior with clean waste.

"Boxing gloves," he said when he looked up and saw me. They set the cocks and watched them fly at each other. I couldn't follow the confusion of wings, but after two or three flies, Erbert grabbed his bird and held him, struggling, while the boy picked up his red and carried it away. Erbert called his thanks after him, meanwhile gently soothing the white bird, stroking his breast and thighs.

"Head fighter he is, did you notice? Goes for the eyes. Bet he chews off every comb in the pit." He put the bird back into the pen, reluctantly came into the enginehouse and picked up his broom. By the time I took out Number 26 that evening, the white cock had gone to roost after his nightcap of bread and port.

It was a misty night, and most of the time I was running blind. When we swooped down into the valleys, where the fog lay in patches, I couldn't see a yard ahead. It was a desolate feeling to be in the handsome walnut cab alone, rushing into the fog, keeping up the speed, my ears stretched and every nerve taut. I wondered if Danny, who was firing in the back cab, felt lonesome too, or if he was thinking about the snakes he wanted to raise on his mythical reptile farm.

As we roared by the dim stations and I hung out, straining to see the lights, I tried to keep my mind on something concrete. The milk-white cock would do. I saw him gobbling barley, looking at me with superb indifference in those bold, inimical eyes. Erbert's enthusiasm had fanned mine, and I was so confident the bird would win that I boasted about his chances to everyone on the road.

When I brought in the empties early the next afternoon, I hung around until it was time to catch the last passenger to the Junction, curious to see what Erbert was about. Today was tailoring day. Erbert retired to the pen, settled himself on his box and held the white cock between his knees, while he sawed off the bird's spurs with the smallest of the metal saws that Hennessey had made for us. After stroking the cock, who responded to caresses with the pleased indifference of a cat, he cut back the magnificent tail a couple of inches and pulled a few feathers from around the vent. Then he washed the yellow legs and long straight toes in a pan of water warmed in the sun.

We had to tell Fred about His Nibs, as Erbert had named the bird; so we all went out to look at him scratching in a corner, covering the yellow legs with a film of dirt. I felt sorry for Erbert's wasted bath, but he looked at the creature with doting eyes.

"Good for him to scratch," he told us. "Fine exercise for the toes."

Erbert told us that it looked as if the gate would be good. When I went across the yard to catch my train, Fred walked over with me. He wasn't particularly pleased to have His Nibs in the back yard, but it was for only two or three more days; so he promised to let the old man alone, if he did his work.

The next day Erbert sponged the cock's head with vinegar and water and gave him a cup of warm bread and milk for a laxative. His afternoon training was "flirting," tossing the bird above a wheelbarrow-load of straw that he had brought from home, spread on the floor and covered with an old horse blanket. Holding the wings and thighs with both hands, Erbert tossed His Nibs into the air, tilting him slightly backward, so that he would have to use his muscles to regain his feet. A dozen times Erbert tossed. He was as serious and careful as a trainer giving John L. Sullivan a workout. Then he ran the bird backward and forward exactly twelve times, before carrying him to the pen.

I got into the habit of staying late or coming early, to be in at the training period. The next afternoon, the day His Nibs got chopped egg added to his barley, Erbert began the leg-strengthening exercises that were his own invention. He put the bird on one end of a four-foot board, which he balanced like a see-saw on his knee, and bounced him up and down by hitting the other end with his fist.

"Did you bring the glove?" Erbert asked me on the day of the fight. He was sitting by the pen with his finger around the white cock's neck, pushing back his neck feathers and trimming them the way a barber cuts hair. After he finished the neck, he trimmed the comb down in a close semicircle and let His Nibs hop down to gobble it.

"Will this do?" I tossed him one of Mamie's old white kid gloves that had a tear in it. As a matter of fact, it was one of her wedding gloves, and I had asked her if she didn't want to put it away in lavender or whatever women use; but she said she had worn it out and it was the thinnest kid she had. Anyway, she wanted to bring us good luck. Erbert caught it on the point of his scissors and felt it.

"That's the very thing to wrap his spurs." After he returned His Nibs to the cage, he cut several thin strips of kid and put them in a cigar box. In this box he had also packed the cock's new steel spurs, a small medicine bottle of sherry, and a package of bread crumbs, together with an apple and an onion for a last snack before the battle. He took the empty water saucer out of the pen (the bird must have no drink this day) and went in to boil the egg for his dinner. When it was hard and cold, he crumbled a quarter of the white for the cock and stuffed the rest into his own mouth.

Erbert wouldn't have shown emotion if he had been expecting to be stretched on the rack; but there was a tension about the place, which increased during the afternoon as boys drifted in solemnly to tell Erbert that their cocks were in fighting condition.

It was Fred's night off, and he had gone to Utica. I had to take out the milk at nine, but Erbert had set the time for the meet at eight o'clock prompt; so I could see a few minutes of it. All afternoon he kept walking about the pen and staring at His Nibs, coming back every few minutes to the engine where I was working.

"I've been feeding him at night to get him accustomed to lantern light." Erbert picked up a piece of waste and began to polish the brass latticework of the brackets holding the headlight. Then out he went again.

"These spurs are the finest made." He lifted them from the cigar box and let me feel the edges. "Fellow I used to work for in England had a silver pair, belonged to his grandfather."

For dinner Erbert cooked mulligan in an old brass kettle we kept on the stove, a few corn nubbins, a handful of pig potatoes, and a soup bone that his nephew (who lived on an adjoining farm) had brought from home. Nobody wanted to leave the place and go into the village to eat. By seven o'clock we were packed into the nephew's wagon, in which the man had promised to rush Dan and me to the enginehouse by nine o'clock. Erbert sat up front on the high seat, with the white cockerel in a sack on his lap and the cigar box beside him, while Dan and I and a couple of boys from the village bounced around in the straw.

The barn was not more than a mile out of town. It smelled of fresh lumber and the summer's crop of hay. There was a full moon, and outside it was almost as light as day. Dan and I stood by Tad Watkins, a section boss from Bridgewater, who was gatekeeper, and tried to estimate the crowd—handlers with their cocks in bags or baskets, farmers who had driven into the meadow and tied their horses to the rail fence, and railroad men from every station this side of Binghamton. A four-horse tallyho, the one that took passengers to the lake landing, dashed up and unloaded guests from the Springs House: sporting gentlemen with bowler hats and walking sticks. Dan nudged me and said that the one with the diamond horseshoe in his scarf was Mr. Vanderbilt.

Old Dad Burr rolled out of a farmer's wagon with Sitting Bull, Gander Schnell, and Bill Tiffany. It looked to me as if every shack was there, and every fireman who had shared a cab with me—even one-eyed Mike, the victim of the ammonia bottle.

When the crowd had gathered, we paid our fifty cents and went inside. The boys had built a real pit, twenty feet wide and over a foot high. They had covered the floor with tanbark and padded the inside of the pit wall with old burlap and horse blankets. Suspended from ropes stretched from loft to loft were fifteen or twenty lanterns, which made a yellow pool in the center of the barn floor and lit up the wisps of dried grass hanging from the dark lofts above, which were bursting with hay.

We walked around the edge of the crowd and found Erbert in a corner, under a wooden yoke for oxen, giving His Nibs a peck or two of the apple and the onion. He took the bread crumbs out of the cigar box, poured them into a saucer and doused them with sherry.

"Here, your Nibs, get a good strong snifter." His Nibs, still dazed by the ride in the sack, arched his white neck and stretched his toes.

"Cocks to the pit!" the referee shouted from the middle of the circle. He was a big farmer from Cedarville.

"Take your time, Your Grace. They've got to examine the spurs." Erbert never got familiar with His Nibs. Not one of us would have thought of calling him "old boy" or "pal."

While the handlers were passing before the referee, showing their spurs, we hurried to the pitside to find a place. When the birds were equally spaced around the ring, we counted forty-seven. Erbert stood directly in front of us, and from the crook of his elbow His Nibs gave us a contemptuous stare. At last the cocks were in position—grays and reds, Dorkings and Pyles, highstationed and lowstationed, with their cropped combs pointing to the wall and their tails to the center of the pit.

"Go!" The handlers freed their birds and hunched down on their heels around the outer edge of the pit. From that moment until the victors were narrowed down to two or three, no one could touch the cocks except Sam Remson, the express agent at Bridgewater, who had been appointed to remove the dead birds from the pit.

In an instant the air was full of slashing spurs and beaks and flashing wings. The battle was too furious and confused for the eye to follow, but I could see flashes of white feathers in the smother of gray and black, and knew that His Nibs was holding on. Back and forth Sam pushed through the crowd, carrying basketfuls of slaughtered birds to the wheelbarrow behind the barn. Sometimes he leaned over to right a cock that was helpless on its back, but no other handling was permitted.

Finally the battle narrowed down to five. His Nibs then slashed a red cock in the lungs at the same moment that a black finished a gray with a broken wing. His Nibs was reeling, and his milk-white hackles, that stood out like a ruff, were splotched with blood—his own or his victims', I couldn't tell. The black cock stalked away a few feet and stood with his wicked eyes on the third, ready to strike the gray, which was sitting lopsided on a broken leg, alive but blinked in both eyes. The referee, with his eyes on his watch, called "sixty seconds," but not a cock stirred.

"Handle," he ordered. Erbert and the handlers of the other two cocks leaped into the pit and returned to their corners, nursing their birds. For thirty seconds Erbert fondled His Nibs, pressing his legs up under him, rubbing his hocks and joints, working his legs back and forth, cleaning his eyes and blowing in his face. Before the referee called the cocks into the pit, the gray was dead. The battle was between the black cock and His Nibs.

Erbert and the other handler carried the exhausted birds to the center, where they feebly pecked at each other, and set them down. Wearily the birds rose into the air—both high fighters, striking for the head.

"Blinked," shouted the crowd. The Black had gouged out His Nibs' left eye. The blood dripped over his white breast feathers, but he had slashed his enemy in the throat. For a few seconds they clung together as they fell on the tanbark.

"Handle?" demanded Erbert. The referee nodded.

Someone was digging his fingers into my arm.

"Come on. We've got ten minutes." It was Danny opening a way for me through the crowd. I looked back to get a last view of Erbert nursing His Nibs' blinded eye with his tongue.

The farmer boy had already untied the horse, and the wagon bumped over the ruts, squeaking as if it were falling apart. We had made arrangements with one of the shacks to build up the fire. He had Number 26 steaming. We tied on our milk cars and pulled out ten minutes late.

It was a clear night, and we soon made up the time with a little extra speed in handling the milk cans stacked on platforms beside the track. All the way to Binghamton, in our separate cabs, we kept thinking about the chances of His Nibs; but we couldn't learn what happened until we got to Norwich on the return trip in the morning. Pulling empties, we didn't get the highball then and had to wait over at Norwich for a passenger; so we planted ourselves at the counter of the railroad restaurant and shouted to Santa Claus. On the stool next to me I saw Andy Ferguson, who had been at the meet and was dead-heading on a coal train to his farm near the Grecian Bend. His eyes were bloodshot, but not from booze—Andy was never a drinking man—and I noticed that the hand around his coffee mug was blistered.

"Who won?" I asked him. "Tell me about the finish."

"Haven't you heard?" He took a gulp of hot coffee, and I could see that he was pretty well played out. "The barn caught fire and burned to the ground. The farmer lost everything, the hay and all. Careless smoking, I reckon. We worked all night with a bucket brigade, but the well was half a mile away, and we couldn't save a thing. Then we passed the hat and collected eleven dollars and fifty cents."

Danny leaned over to hear. "You don't say. Imagine a bunch of ding-dongs having eleven dollars and fifty cents after the betting closed."

"Yeah," Andy sighed. "It was pretty tough on Erbert. There wasn't anything for him to do but chip in with his winnings."

Then His Nibs had won! After the big news of the fire, Andy told us about the battle. It looked as though Erbert's cock was a goner, with both eyes blinked and a wing broken; but he wouldn't lie down and die. As he made a last, lopsided effort to strike, he fell over on his back, practically dead. Erbert, the canny lad, didn't leap to handle him, and the other handler didn't bother to pick up the black cock but kept shouting, "Attaboy, you done it, Attaboy."

The black cock strutted about the pit, then walked over to His Nibs and raised his head to crow. But with the first note of victory, the white cockerel shot up his claw, slashed the black in the lungs and dropped him stone dead. His Nibs lived long enough to be the champion.

19. The Killer

THE ENGINEHOUSE WAS A PIT OF GLOOM after the fight. Erbert moped around with a greasy handful of waste, looking as if it was hardly worth while to go jump in the lake; and Fred was too annoyed with the whole business to toss the old fellow a cheerful word. When the new reflector for the headlight came from the factory, Erbert was broke, of course; and so was Fred, who had to pay not only for the light but for the handsome chime whistle that he had installed on the engine. It had four notes, and he was just beginning to master the first four bars of *Yankee Doodle.*

One afternoon when I came across from the station and found Fred in the stall packing a tank journal, he looked up and gave me a rueful grin.

"See, the eagle got knocked off the top of the bell. Either Number 26 is hoodooed or I am. Maybe it's both of us. We sure do play in bad luck."

I remembered what he had said, later that fall, when she ran over a man near Bridgewater. I was bringing in the empties, making time on the home stretch, when Danny, who had his head out of the window of the back cab, let out a shriek. I threw her into the big hole just in time to see a man topple over the high embankment.

Gander Schnell, the conductor, was off almost as soon as we were. Quick in an emergency, he had two shacks out protecting before the rest of us reached the foot of the bank and the crumpled bundle that lay there—a man, not mangled but apparently quite dead.

The brakeman got a ladder from the caboose (we carried no stretcher in those days), and the four of us lifted the body onto it as gently as we could. Climbing up the embankment was a job for a monkey. Gander and I held the foot of the ladder shoulder high, and Danny and the shack climbed backward, bent over, with the ladder no higher than their knees. About halfway up, someone's foot slipped. The man fell off, rolled down the bank and, as he hit the ditch, regained a moment of consciousness.

When Danny heard groans coming from what he considered a lifeless body, he dropped the ladder and scrambled to the track, frightened as a rabbit. He hid somewhere in the tender, and we saw no more of him until the three of us had laid the man on the caboose floor and I had whistled in the flags. Brave as a wildcat when he was facing anything alive, Danny was full of Irish superstition about the dead; and when he came out of the coal to stoke the fire, his eyes were popping.

We took the body to the Springs and next morning at the inquest were cleared of negligence, because the man was a local half-wit, notoriously unable to take care of himself. The accident was no fault of ours, but it gave us the creeps. Maybe Fred was right about the hoodoo.

He was driving the unpredictable old girl when she struck again—rammed the rear end of Number 6 one cold day at Wood's Corner, and injured a woman and her baby. Fred claimed Number 6 had not sent out flags; but on account of his previous record he was taken off the road and made inspector of engines in the roundhouse.

But Fred had guts; he didn't let his run of bad luck get him down. He was still one of the best engineers on the division, and he held up his head, even though it tore his vitals to spend his days checking over engines that the other fellows brought in. There is something depressing about a cold engine; it is almost like a dead thing unless you are working on it.

Everybody inside and out of the roundhouse liked Fred and believed that his bad luck was all traceable to Number 26. They began to call her "the killer" and prophesied that the Old Man was going to have a hard time getting anyone to run her when she came out of the shop. The engineers never let up on Tom Thatcher about Fred, and they may have been right—that the engine was hoodooed and not the man; for after he got back on the road, Fred never had another accident. He lived long enough to win the highest seniority rating, and died running one of the best trains on the division.

All this talk about Number 26 made me a little nervous, but I told myself it was silly to be superstitious. While she was being patched up, I was in the dumps. I was lonesome without Fred and felt depressed every time I saw him in the enginehouse. When 26 returned from the shop, I wanted a change and was glad when the Old Man told me to try her out on extra passenger for a few days before putting her back on the milk.

She was almost as handsome as ever, except for the fine headlight that Fred had bought. The fluted brass brackets that held it were not replaced, and the ordinary headlight had no artwork on the sides. Her walnut cab had been re-varnished to hide the scratches, and she was spruce and gleaming. It was ridiculous to pin a hoodoo on the shining old gal.

I was marked up to pull Number 11, the late passenger to Richfield Springs, while the regular engineer was out with the grippe. So I took her to the Junction to pick up the parlor car from Binghamton. She ran like an antelope. Her valves had been set, her paint cleaned, her whole works overhauled, and she had such a good pickup that she took North Bridgewater hill almost as easily as she rolled along on the level.

It was late October, and dark before we got in. The fireman, who lived in the village, got off at the station, came front to tell me that it was a pretty run and said good night. I dropped the cars and ran Number 26 into one of the two stalls in the enginehouse. I was turning her over to the new wiper, Tony (An Italian, who had re-placed Erbert), when Ed Haight brought in his freight engine and rolled her into the other stall.

"Joe," he asked me, "did you run over something this side of South Columbia?" This was the first station out of Richfield Springs. I hadn't seen anything, but he was sure he had passed over a sheep or a dog on the track, or it might have been a man.

"Oh, well," he said, "if you didn't see anything, maybe I was wrong. Good night." He lit his lantern and went off across the yard. With my torch I looked over the front of the engine and the pilot, and got down on my hands and knees and threw the beam underneath; but my hand was so unsteady that the point of light shimmied like a firefly in the swamp. I was certain that 26 had killed again.

In the brake rigging of the tank was part of a man's head.

"Look here, Tony," I said to the wiper, who was crouching beside me, staring at the finger of light moving over the oily pattern of machinery. "Get me the hose and we'll wash it off." But when Tony realized that he was looking at a piece of human head, he leaped to his feet with such violence that I could hear his knees crack.

"No! No! Not for a thousand dollars! No. Won't go near Goddamned engine." He rushed out of the shed as if the devil were after him. That was the last we ever saw of Tony.

I was alone and couldn't leave the engine, so I got the section boss to take a handcar and go down the track to investigate. He found what was left of a man and notified the coroner, who held me for an inquest in the morning. That night I had to stay in the shed and watch the engine. It was like keeping guard over a sleeping murderer.

The inquest was short. The man was, according to the coroner's description, "a common drunk," who had been seen going down the track about an hour before we were due. He was a trespasser, and there was no cause for action. Even if it had been broad daylight, I would not have been able to stop in time to save him. In the enginehouse and shop at Utica the men shook their heads and muttered about "the killer," but I didn't believe Number 26 could be held accountable for running over a drunk and a half-wit. Such accidents could have happened to any engineer and any engine.

In broad daylight, common sense told me that the old girl had just run into a streak of hard luck. I put the whole matter out of my mind and steamed out confidently a few days later when we were sent to Binghamton to bring in Number 3, the afternoon passenger. We left Binghamton at 3:35 and were due in Utica at 6:20, where we connected with the New York Central express that was scheduled fifteen minutes later. It was a connection that we tried to make, come hell or high water, for the superintendent considered it a disgrace to the Lackawanna if one of our trains stabbed another line.

Sitting Bull was the conductor, recently promoted to the passenger service. When he came front to the cab and handed me the orders, he looked like an admiral in his freshly pressed blue uniform and brass buttons. The boys around the enginehouse said he was so proud of the uniform that he all but slept in it, and could hardly wait until dusk to light the coach lamps and show it off. He looked curiously at Number 26.

"She looks right smart to me. Give her the works, Joe; we want to get in on the dot."

We made good time to the Junction, but there luck was against us, and we lost twenty minutes transferring an unusually heavy load of passengers and baggage. Sitting Bull came forward before he gave us the highball, anxiously rubbing the face of his watch with his thumb.

"What do you think, kid, can you pick it up?"

I nodded. Anyway, I was going to try. Making up speed on the thirteen miles of downgrade to Utica, through six little mill and factory villages and over a number of unprotected highway crossings, was a blood-freezing business. But we had no scheduled stops, and it could be done if a runner kept his nerve and let her travel. I gave Number 26 the gun to start her from the Junction, then shut off the steam and let her roll. In a few minutes we were running at sixty miles an hour, shrieking past the stations and over the crossings. It was twilight and beginning to drizzle. I hung out, with the rain in my face, squinting down the track.

Between Chadwick's Mills and Washington Mills was a grade crossing where a highway ran diagonally across the track, making it difficult to see anything coming from the left, especially in a double-cab engine. Giving the regular warning, two long blasts and two short, I looked to right and left and saw nothing; but suddenly, about fifty feet from the crossing a horse's head shot in front of the left window, then the top of a buggy. Automatically I threw the brake valve into the big hole, but at sixty miles an hour we couldn't stop under a thousand feet. The next second came the crash. The impact smashed in the front window, splattering me with glass and wood and torn flesh.

Before we had come to a stop, I was on the track. I must have been a repulsive sight, torn and splattered with blood.

Sitting Bull was out of the head coach and followed me to the engine, still clutching a five-dollar bill and a handful of change. I ran to the pilot and saw the wreckage of a horse and carriage. The remains of the driver, a young man, we found wedged between the smokebox and the pilot, his head severed from his body.

The passengers milled around Sitting Bull, making themselves a nuisance with their advice and threats against the railroad company; but he kept his head. The best thing we could do, he thought, was to get on as quickly as possible.

"Call in your flag, Joe," he directed. "We will put the baggageman and fireman on the pilot to watch the body and move slowly to Washington Mills Station, where we can wire Utica."

At the Mills we got word from the superintendent to remove the body, leave it in care of the agent and proceed to Utica. It was a gruesome job, separating the body from the engine, especially with the jostling and advice of the passengers; but we did the best we could and were soon rolling. The cab was a shambles. The rain beat in the front window and wet me to the skin, but I figured that it might wash off some of the stains.

The superintendent was waiting for us at the station.

"How fast were you running, Joe?" he asked me.

"About sixty miles," I told him.

"Don't let it worry you." He put his hand on my shoulder. "We have a right to run at any speed within the rules of the company, and we are responsible for any damage done to persons or their property when they are within their rights. Go on home and don't let it get you down." A grand fellow, Salsbury; he always stuck by his men.

When I reached home and came in through the kitchen door, Mamie gave me one look and began to sob; but when she saw that I wasn't really hurt, she stopped crying and told me to get out of my clothes before my supper was spoiled. When I came back into the kitchen with my face washed and the scratches covered with plasters, she poured the coffee.

"Don't think about it," she said, when I told her what had happened. "You didn't do anything wrong, and you couldn't help it." She stacked my plate with golden fried potatoes that smelled like heaven.

"There," she said, running her fingers over my wet hair. "Isn't it good? But Joe, I wish you'd ask the Old Man to give you another engine."

"That's all bosh," I answered hotly. "There's nothing the matter with Number 26."

"Nothing," snapped Mamie, "except she's a killer and everybody knows it. I wish you were off of her."

She poured me another cup of coffee and gave me a piece of cake (the kind her mother always kept on the sideboard in Carthage), and we said no more about the accident. When I went to take Number 26 out in the morning, she was as sleek as ever. The wipers had worked on her all night, washing her down and replacing the broken windows. Although I was jittery all the way, it was an uneventful trip—everywhere on time, everything going like clockwork. The only thing unusual was the telegram that the operator gave us at Norwich, on the way home: a notice ordering the whole crew to attend the inquest at Washington Mills in the morning.

When we got in that afternoon, in good time for the New York Central connection, and ran Number 26 onto the turntable, Bill Tiffany, in on a coal train, came across to the engine. As I climbed down, he waved the evening paper under my nose. I put out my hand to steady it and read the headlines marching across the page in heavy black capitals. "TWO KILLED AT WILLOWVALE CROSSING." The engine foreman came over with another paper, and the boys all crowded around.

"Two prominent citizens," read one of the wipers over Bill's shoulder. "What did you do with the other? We thought it was only one."

". . . inhuman attitude of the railway employees, who never took the trouble to look in what remained of the carriage and left the driver's companion lying undiscovered in the ditch."

"Oh, boy, this is serious," said Tiffany. "You'll have a riot up there tomorrow, considering how the farmers already hate the railroads."

I grabbed the paper and read it myself.

"Where's Sitting Bull?" asked one of the engineers. "Wait until he sees this!" But he had gone home and was probably reading about it as he ate his supper.

The situation did look black. We should have searched the ditches, but the horror of the catastrophe under our eyes was so overpowering, and we were so busy trying to handle it the right way, that it didn't occur to a single one of us, crew or passengers, to look for another person.

Bill Tiffany gave me a kindly push.

"Go on home and get a good supper. You'll need your wits about you tomorrow. I'm going to stick around and tell old Dad Burr when he gets in. He'll be all cut up about Sitting Bull. Funny how those two used to claw at each other."

In the morning Mamie gave me my dinner pail and a hug that nearly strangled me.

"There's an extra piece of apple pie for you. Now don't you worry, it will come out all right. Just tell them exactly what happened. You didn't do anything wrong."

We all deadheaded on the morning passenger: the fireman, the express messenger, the baggageman, the two shacks, and Sitting Bull, who had evidently spent the night cleaning and pressing his uniform. He held himself so straight and looked so impressive with his silver hair and whiskers above the gold buttons, that we all felt a little easier.

"Don't fret, Joe," he whispered to me. "The section foreman and the agent at Washington Mills have canvassed the whole Willowvale district, and they found plenty of witnesses to testify that you whistled at the crossing." That made me feel better. I knew that I had, but all night I lay awake wondering how I could prove it.

At Washington Mills the coroner's jury was waiting for us on the platform: twelve men, kept well in hand by the coroner, a brisk and courteous old German doctor who seemed to know his business. My eyes roved hurriedly over the jury. Not all of them were farmers, thank heaven; a few had the lighter tan of the mill workers.

The coroner stepped up to Sitting Bull, whom he judged to be in command of the party, shook hands pleasantly and suggested that we go to the site of the accident, so that the jury would have a better understanding of the circumstances. We all started back along the track to Willowvale crossing. The rain had stopped during the night, and the goldenrod along the edge of the fields was bright in the sun. Sitting Bull and the coroner led the procession. Behind it came a crowd of villagers and farmers, shouting threats against the train crew and the railroad. One old farmer—perhaps a train had killed one of his cows—clumped along beside us, threatening us with his corncob pipe and shouting that the proper thing was to lynch the engineer. It didn't make me feel any more comfortable when a small boy pointed his finger at me, yelling, "That's him, that's him!"

Finally we arrived at the schoolhouse where the inquest was to be held: a big room with blackboards between the windows, covered with sums and copy-book phrases. On one blackboard were childish drawings of a cat, a frog, and a bug, with the names printed after them in high, irregular letters. Everybody crowded in who could squeeze through the door. The farmer who wanted to lynch me was well to the front—so near that I could see the gaps in his tobacco-stained teeth. The coroner kept the front seats cleared for us and the witnesses, and he himself stood by the teacher's desk, pounding for quiet.

In the space around the desk several men in town black, with sheepskin books under their arms, eyed each other sharply or pushed through the crowd to question the relatives of the two dead men.

"Lawyers," whispered Sitting Bull out of the corner of his mouth. "Old ferret-eyes looking for business. Think they scent a juicy case against the company." One of them —"Judge," they called him—a strutter with an overstuffed belly, kept walking around and flirting his coat tail, as if he were the leading actor in the show; but the coroner paid no attention to him. After a preliminary description of the accident, the coroner called me as the first witness and courteously asked me to describe what had happened, in my own words.

Scarcely had I opened my mouth when the "judge" interrupted. In a booming voice, drawing every eye to his portly figure, he demanded, "How long have you been handling steam power?"

I looked at the coroner. Did the man have any right to use my age against me? It wouldn't help to tell them how many years, because they would think I was lying. I knew that I looked even younger than I was.

Before I could answer, the coroner reminded the "judge" that it was an improper question and that no one could question the witness without his permission.

"Go on," he instructed me. "You had no stops between Richfield Junction and Utica, and you were making about sixty miles an hour when you were approaching the crossing. Did you blow the whistle?"

"Yes, I blew the whistle."

"How do you know you blew the whistle?" the "judge" interrupted belligerently.

"You are instructed not to answer that question." Turning on the "judge," his eyes spitting fire, the coroner reminded him that he, the coroner, was holding this inquest and that it was going to be conducted in the manner that

he saw fit. He wished to remind the "judge," as well as the jury and the spectators, that these witnesses were not yet criminals and could not be treated as such. The inquest was not a criminal court, its duty was not to prosecute but to determine the cause of the accident.

The "judge" snorted. For a moment there was a duel of eyes, then the other lawyers leaped to the defense of the "judge," and for a while the court dissolved into a free-for-all between the coroner and the lawyers. As I was on the witness stand, I tried not to appear too interested; but I could see that Sitting Bull was thoroughly enjoying the show. I was afraid that he might let out a cheer for the sturdy little doctor at any moment.

Presently the coroner won out. He had a good pair of lungs, and he wasn't going to let any bunch of accident-chasers push him around. The inquest was resumed in an orderly manner, and there was not a squeak out of the lawyers while we testified—Sitting Bull, the rest of the crew, and the witnesses who had heard the whistle and seen the accident.

It was past noon when the jury retired to the cloak room. I was hungry, and in spite of my belief that I would be cleared, there was a horrid gnawing uneasiness in the pit of my stomach. The old farmer kept staring at me and making the motion of wringing my neck, and there was an angry buzz in the crowd which stuck icicles into my spine.

When the jury came back, we all stood up, I noticed Sitting Bull nervously polishing a button on his cap. The foreman, a big, slow-witted mill hand, began with a rambling comment on the accident. If he was going to take this chance to make a speech, I thought, I would choke him; but the coroner quickly told him to come to the point. The man blushed a dull red that rose clear to his forehead and beaded it with perspiration. He had a bad case of stage fright, but managed to say that the jury exonerated the company of all blame and recommended that a watchman be stationed at the crossing.

We shook hands all around. Then Sitting Bull herded his crew back to the station, where the agent wired the news to Utica. A coal train was cutting off a gondola on the switch and waiting for a meet with the local freight, so we had time to gobble our dinner before we climbed into the caboose. Famished, I cleaned the pail as if I hadn't seen food for a week. While I was stowing away the second piece of pie, the freight came in. The wheels had hardly stopped rolling when Dad Burr dropped to the ground and, moving lightly for all the flesh he carried, came over to the platform where we were waiting in the sun behind the freight house.

Stretching out his right hand to Sitting Bull and his left to me, he beamed at us.

"I can see you got a clean slate. My God, kid, you sure did have us worried. We thought we might have to break you out of the cooler and give you a waybill for Texas or Mexico."

While his new conductor unloaded, old Sheep-face and I stretched out our legs on the platform and had a smoke. Sitting Bull balanced uncomfortably on a narrow box, because he didn't want to get his pants dusty. It was so comfortable and friendly and reassuring that if I had been a kid I would have bawled with happiness.

20. Mainliner

THE OLD MAN WAS PRETTY DECENT TO ME after the inquest. He called me in and said, "Joe, are you afraid of Number 26? If you are, say so, and I'll take you off the milk." Was I going to let that engine get me or wasn't I? Now was the time to make up my mind whether I was going to be a superstitious numbskull or use what intelligence the Lord had given me. Looking the Old Man straight in the eye, I answered, "No, Mr. Thatcher, I don't think there's a thing wrong with her."

"All right," he said. "I don't either. Take her back on the milk. You're senior engineer on the job—God forgive me for robbing the cradle—and remember you have one of the fastest trains on the road."

The Old Man loved Number 26 almost as much as Fred did. There was a trace of affection in his voice whenever he spoke of her.

So I went back on the milk. Number 26 and I made the night run for four years without a mishap, and after I left her, she never figured in a serious accident. Maybe my determination to have no fear of her tamed her for good, I don't know. She pulled the milk for a long time, until she in her turn was too light; but she never suffered the indignity of demotion to odd jobs, dragging work trains or snubbing empties around the yard. Years later, when I was spending an afternoon off, fishing in the Chenango, I saw her pass over the trestle "light," headed for Binghamton; and I had a queer, sad feeling that she was on her way to Scranton to the junk pile. The boys said it was true, and that she had gone gallantly under her own power.

The milk run was a good one; every third day off, with one night over at the Springs. I didn't see the Old Man often or spend much time around the office and shops, because Number 26 rarely came in to Utica. At first I missed the friendliness and the gossip; but I was settling down, paying for the house, putting a little money away in the bank for emergencies (now that I had two young sons to look after), and saving my extra runs, not for a flier on the cocks or a big night at John Collins', but for a trip to England.

My brother Alfred and I had promised each other that, when we could manage it, we would go back to the village in Kent which had been our home and visit our sister, whom we barely remembered. When I had accumulated enough money from extra runs, Alfred too had money in the savings bank, and we figured that between us we could squeeze the necessary jack. Mamie was occupied with the children, so she told us to go by ourselves, if we could get leave, and have a good time. It was the first real vacation for either of us.

I counted on Old Tom's softening up a little, because he was an Englishman himself; so I asked him for a sixty-day leave and a letter stating that I was a good engineer employed by him on the Lackawanna. With the letter I intended to see what I could do about getting free transportation on the British railroads.

"I'm not sure about that 'good engineer' stuff," he said, "but I'll be glad to get rid of you for sixty days." He came through with a fine letter, painstakingly written in his own crabbed hand.

On the boat I met an upstanding old Englishman, an engine "driver" (as the English call their engineers) from the London, Midland & Scottish Railway, who was returning from a sightseeing tour of the United States as the guest of Chauncey Depew. Once he had pulled Mr. Depew's special train over his road; and at the end of the run the president of the New York Central came to the engine and thanked him. He complimented Mr. Higginbottom on the smooth run, and promised him that, if he should ever come to the United States, he should have free transportation to the Pacific Coast and back. Mr. Higginbottom didn't forget the invitation. He saved the passage money to New York and looked up Mr. Depew. As good as his word, the Senator arranged for a round trip to the Coast, with stopovers at all the points of interest; so the old gentleman was coming home with an eyeful of America.

This was music to my ears. If he had fared so handsomely on American railroads, maybe I would have luck with the English roads. Taking out of my vest pocket the letter from Mr. Thatcher, I showed it to him and asked what chance he thought I'd have of getting passes in England. The old man shook his head. He had never heard of such a thing. Still, it wouldn't hurt to try. The superintendent was the man to see.

"And, lad," he advised me, "when you go into his office, take off your hat and don't talk too loud. When I was in America, I heard some of the most shocking language from the engineers and enginemasters. A chap couldn't get away with such rude language in England." I wondered what he would have thought if he had heard the Old Man.

Regretfully I said good-by to Mr. Higginbottom at the dock. He got off at Liverpool, and we were going on to Hastings, where our sister and her husband were proprietors of a damp, cold, and historic old inn named "The Fortunes of War." After seeing Battle Abbey and the other relics of William the Conqueror, I went to Staplehurst, the little village in which I was born. I found the old house at one end of the main street and the duck pond at the other all unchanged, except that the pond had shrunk to a puddle, and I remembered it as the size of Lake Erie.

One member of my family was left: the niece who was older than I and used to give me scones and jam. After twenty-five years, she had finally married her William, and they were spending their belated honeymoon in her parents' home, which had been the scene of his long and faithful courtship. She fitted into the past as if there had been no gap in time; but my sister was a stranger. We found no common ground on which to renew the old affection, although we tried. Perhaps the cold had something to do with my unresponsiveness. Not one comfortable moment did I spend in the inn. My teeth chattered, my bones ached and I nearly fell to pieces with the ague, even wrapped in my overcoat and with a scarf tied around my throat. If it hadn't been for the warmth of good English stout, I should have turned blue and petrified, like a fish on ice.

After a few days I went up to London, hoping with luck to get a pass to Edinburgh or Glasgow. At the station I walked around to the engine shed and found a driver oiling his wheels. He seemed friendly enough. So after watching him for a few minutes, I told him that I was a driver in America, and that through our superintendents we were able to get transportation for engineers on other roads.

"Well, you can't do it here, mate," he told me. But if I wanted to try, he wished me luck. Jerking his thumb toward the platform, he indicated an elegant gentleman in a high hat.

"He's the superintendent. Go see him. Name's Simpson." I went over to Mr. Simpson, took off my hat (as Mr. Higginbottom had told me to do), introduced myself and gave him Mr. Thatcher's letter. He took me to his office. A whiskered clerk rushed up with a chair, and I sat down by a desk with a little teapot and a cup and saucer on it. Mr. Simpson put a monocle in his eye and looked at me over the teapot.

"What is it I can do for you?"

When he learned that I wanted a pass for either Edinburgh or Glasgow and return, he said that his road had never honored employees of foreign railroads with free transportation, only officials; but he would give me a pass on one of the Scots, second class, as far as York. That was the end of his jurisdiction. A letter to the superintendent at York would get me as far as Berwick, and in that manner I would be passed along from superintendent to superintendent. He asked me to call when I returned to London and tell him what I thought of his railroad.

It was a pleasant trip, stopping over a day at each of the points suggested by Mr. Simpson. On the station platform in Glasgow, as I was waiting for my train to London, one of the guards said to me, "Where to, mate? London? For two bob and a close mouth, I can put you in one of the empty compartments, and you can sleep on one of the long seats all the way to London."

Wanting to learn all that I could about English railroading customs, I gave him the two shillings and settled in the compartment. In a few minutes another two passengers were shown in (two-bobbers also, I guessed). One was a Bill Sykes in the flesh, straight out of Dickens, bundle, short stick, and all; and the other an old gentleman in a clerical coat, with side-whiskers that stuck out very straight and covered his ears. The old gentleman opened the window in the door and began to shout, to anyone who might be listening, that he must have a cup of tea. The tea-vender came to the window, handed up the tea and stood waiting for the cup and saucer, but the clergyman refused to give it back.

"I paid this individual sixpence for this wretched cup of tea," the old man said to me, "and now he wants the cup and saucer, which I shall not give him. It is a souvenir of Glasgow."

The tea-vender protested, with cries and curses; the parson shook his fist, threatened to give the man a jolly good kick in the backside, and rattled the door (which he knew very well was locked). The guard blew his whistle and the train pulled out. All this fascinated me, it was so different from the way we do things on the Lackawanna.

When I called to thank Mr. Simpson for his courtesy, I told him how well I liked the English trains: the coaches rode smoother and with less noise than ours in America. And what did I think about the English locomotives? he asked. Although I had not ridden in one, I was bound to say that I didn't like them as well as ours.

"I expected you to say that," commented Mr. Simpson, giving me a cool stare through his monocle. "Your Yankee idea of an engine is a lot of pipes sticking about, a cowcatcher on the front and, last but by no means least, a church bell on the top."

When I got home, I told Mr. Thatcher about the shops of the Southeastern & Chatham Railway, which I had visited in Hastings—everything neat and clean as a New England kitchen, no old pieces of wheels or pistons or cylinder heads piled about, flower beds in the yard, gardeners to take care of them, and roses running up the walls.

Old Tom snorted. "Roses indeed! I bet you two bob they didn't smell as sweet as Scotty Haight."

Before the boys in the roundhouse had forgotten to joke me about railroading with flowers, the Utica Division was cast into gloom by a particularly grievous accident. The engine of Number 6, the crack through passenger, exploded on Paris Hill, killing both the engineer and the fireman. John Keach, the engineer, was one of the oldest and most popular men on the road, and the young fireman was a local boy, whose family lived on a farm near Chenango Forks.

The assignment to trains 9 and 6, which doubled between Utica and Binghamton, was among the best on the road—one of those runs that are generally filled by old engineers, the elder statesmen of the line. These were the plums. If you got one, you were established for life, with nothing likely to remove you except death or discipline. There were a lot of rumors about the vacancy, but I paid very little attention to them. I felt no personal interest, because several engineers older and better qualified than I were in line for promotion.

When I found Daniel Hall, the conductor of 9 and 6, waiting for me one morning in the enginehouse at Binghamton, I was surprised. He was one of the old-timers who were generally pleasant enough to a kid but never hung around to talk. It was four o'clock, a grisly hour in the morning, not the time one would choose for a chat.

"Come over to the nightowl lunch and have a cup of coffee," he said. "It's my day off, and I thought I'd stick around and see you."

When we were sitting on the high stools, alone except for the sleepy quick-order cook and a couple of shacks at the other end of the counter, Mr. Hall asked me what I would think about taking John Keach's run. I didn't answer him seriously, for there were too many ahead of me; but he pointed out that the three or four men who were qualified for the run lived in Utica. Some of them owned their own houses, and others objected to getting up at three o'clock in the morning to take out Number 9.

"You'd have to move to Binghamton," said Dan, "but you ought to do that anyway, for the sake of your wife and the children. You know that the runners of the best passengers, the cream of the road, live here. If you stay in Utica, you'll be the callboy all your life."

I was too dazed to thank him properly for his advice; but deadheading home on the cushions I kept thinking about it, wondering why Dan had picked me and whether he had put in a word for me with the Old Man. It wasn't until years later that he told me how he had suggested me to the superintendent, afraid some grouch would get the run.

I had always admired Dan; he would be a good running partner. Altogether it was a big chance, but I wasn't at all sure what Mamie would think about it. That night we talked it over. I asked her how she would feel about leaving her church and her friends and the house we were buying. She didn't hesitate a minute; she was all for taking it.

The next day the Old Man sent for me and minced no words. "How would you like trains 9 and 6?"

While I was hesitating, not wanting to seem too anxious, he made up my mind for me.

"I am not monkeying with a lot of damn fool engineers. You will go out on Number 6 tomorrow and like it."

I thanked him and said I had always wanted the run but

never thought he would give it to me; and since he had, I hoped he would start me off with a good engine.

"You will take what I give you, and the first break you make, you are out on your ear. Smoke that up." The Old Man wasn't going to let my promotion go to my head.

The next day when I went over to the ready track to get the engine for Number 6, I saw that Old Tom had given me a good steamer. I had run her once or twice and knew that she stepped along at a lively pace. At Oxford, where we passed the milk on the siding, the whole crew were standing by the track wiping their eyes with their handkerchiefs. I waved back and pretended to wring the tears from mine, too; and the gesture was not all in fun. Four years we had fought and lied and covered for each other, and these things make ties that are hard to break.

So Mamie and I moved to Binghamton in the spring of '97, and I settled into the new schedule: up at three, to take out Number 9 at 4:15 with the Pullmans from New York, arrive at Utica at 8 in the morning, catch a cup of coffee and bacon and eggs and exchange the news with the boys in the enginehouse, out at 11:05 and into Binghamton at 1:40 in the afternoon.

At first I was not exactly welcomed in the Binghamton enginehouse with the banging of cymbals and blowing of trumpets. The older engineers and the runners on the main line who ran out of Binghamton to Syracuse, Buffalo, Hoboken, looked upon me as a boy from the sticks who had to be kept in his place.

The enginehouse was crowded and there weren't enough stalls for all the engines that laid over, so some of them had to stand out in the weather on the service track. My predecessor, John Keach, had a regular stall, which I had expected to inherit; but when I went down on the first morning, I was surprised to find the engine for Number 9 out on the service track.

The engine foreman was standing near-by, watching me, but he didn't say a word. I hesitated, but I couldn't let this go by—if I was going to let myself be put upon first off, my life would be deviled out of me—so I told him I understood that the Utica Division was assigned two stalls, one of them for the engine of Numbers 9 and 6. He had talked the matter over with some of the older engineers, the foreman said, and they were of the opinion that the stall should go to Tom Niles on the Scranton milk. Tom had spoken for it, and as he was older in the service, it was going to him instead of a new engineer from the sticks.

"Well," I said, in the most impressive tone I could muster, "Mr. Thatcher will have something to say about this."

"Tom Thatcher is not running the Binghamton end of your job," he answered, getting nasty. "But go right ahead if you want to make trouble for yourself on your first trip."

All the way to Utica I thought of the best way to get the Old Man's dander up. When I got in, I went over to the office and repeated the conversation to Tom, emphasizing the foreman's boast that at Binghamton Tom Thatcher had no authority over his own engines.

"He did, did he!" The glass eye revolved toward me like a beacon in a gale. "By God, we'll see. I'll go down with you on Number 6 and see Mr. Halstead in Scranton, and when I get back to Binghamton you can have the whole enginehouse if you want it."

Old Tom had a drag with Halstead, who had been his friend and idol since the days when they were young on the road together. Halstead was a bluff, tough old fellow who had started as a water boy and worked his way up to General Manager by sheer ability. The men liked him, because he was straight and lived only for the D. L. and W., but they weren't so fond of the under-officials who aped his ways.

When Old Tom got back to Binghamton, he had his vocabulary all polished off and was spoiling for a fight. His personal opinion of the foreman and everyone connected with him, and his prophecies of what would happen to them if they showed any further discrimination against his men, would have sizzled an asbestos plate. The foreman said that I could have the stall and fry in hell for all he cared.

In the morning the engine was in the house, but I could see that I had not increased my popularity with the older engineers by calling in Mr. Thatcher and Mr. Halstead. The next day I met Tom Niles: a big man, about two hundred and seventy pounds on the hoof, and a bachelor who didn't have to account to anybody for his fights. He looked me over contemptuously and smiled.

"Well, well, I declare, this must be Tommy Thatcher's little boy."

But he let me alone, and in time the other engineers forgot that I was a new runner from the sticks.

Dan Hall had held himself aloof from the tussle for the engine shed, but during my little war for recognition one of my stanchest supporters was Pat Grace, the baggage-man. He had come to the Utica Division at about the time I was set up with an engine, we were of about the same age and the same mind, had the same number of children, and were fast friends from the beginning. Pat had run on Numbers 6 and 9 for several years and abetted me in trying to make as good a record if not better than that of John Keach, who was reputed to make the smoothest stops and the steadiest runs of the division.

At the end of the run, I got into the habit of stopping at the baggage car and asking Pat how she rode the curves.

"A little ragged in some places," he would answer. "You know, Joe, I think Keach didn't take them so fast," or "He touched them up a little with the air. I can tell by the way my baggage rides."

We talked endlessly about the best way to take curves without checking the speed. My ambition was to run smoothly, like Keach, without losing time; and I figured that it could be done by slowing on the approaches to curves and letting out the steam on the actual curves to prevent the slack from running out. We arranged for Pat to keep a pail of water on the floor of the baggage car and note the places at which it spilled. In that way he helped me to ease over the rough spots.

One day when I had made up time on Number 9, I asked Pat how she came through this morning.

"Joe," he said, "I could have shaved a sleeping mouse and not waked him all the way." He never lost a chance to give me an encouraging word, and with his help I worked out the best way to get up maximum speed as quickly as possible without jerking the train. Between us we kept up Keach's reputation for the smoothest ride on the division.

21. Exit the Old Man

IT WAS NO HARDSHIP TO GET UP IN THE DARK, swig a cup of coffee and eat a biscuit on the run, enough to stay me until there was time for eggs and bacon in Utica. And I liked shooting through the final black before daybreak, sitting comfortably on my perch, swaying with the gentle roll of the engine as she took the curves along the Chenango, watching the headlights sweep first one side of the track and then the other. This was the sort of job in which a man could put down roots. Mamie had her friends and her activities, the boys had found playmates on our own street in the pretty little houses overlooking the Chenango, and I spent my holidays shooting and fishing with the Gun and Rod Club.

On my engine, Number 930 (a new speed buggy, one of the latest from Schenectady) rode a handsome brass eagle that Clark & Eberson in Utica had given me when I bought forty-five dollars' worth of ammunition for the club. In a sense this was the first engine that I regarded as my own. The Sable Prince was a handsome one for a hog, but I was always wanting to get off the coal; and Number 26 belonged peculiarly to Fred Willkie and the Old Man.

But Number 930 was mine; in all probability nobody else would drive her. I stuck my son Raymond's picture on the wall and a snapshot of young Leslie, spent my extra-run money for a brass hatchet to top the flag staff and felt that nothing was too good for her.

But just as soon as life settles into a definite pattern and you think that you can foresee what the design will be, something always happens to change it. For five years I had been on the night run, and had begun to feel almost like an old-timer around the enginehouse at Binghamton, when we heard by the stovepipe route that we were going to have a new president and general manager. This was something to gossip about; but in our hearts we did not believe it possible for the D. L. & W. to run without Mr. Sloane and Mr. Halstead.

We did not realize how old-fashioned we were. Each division had its own shops; the engines and coaches were built in the division and no two of them were alike, or even painted the same color; we had no standard operating rules, no standard equipment, no interchangeable parts; each shop had to carry a large overhead of supplies for repairs. But we had always run that way and any other plan seemed unthinkable.

The old-timers worried. We had never been limited in supplies, and the schedule wasn't cut and dried. Often we got a couple of days gratis when the Master Mechanic felt like it. They grumbled at the thought of a reorganization, fearful that all freedom and self-expression were going to be taken out of their lives. But we who were younger were inclined to wait and see.

Mr. Sloane and Mr. Halstead personified the road to me. Every summer I pulled them to Richfield Springs for the races, and Mr. Halstead for a number of week-ends. The President was a short Scotch-Irishman, always dancing and nervous. I never had any direct contact with him; but the General Manager was a hard and notional man to pull. He generally came down from Scranton in the private car, the *Lake Forest*, which I thought at that time the final word in luxury. I brought the car down on Number 6 and was cut off the regular run at the Junction to take it to Richfield Springs. The first time I pulled him, the train dispatcher said to me when he handed me the order, "Here's your schedule for forty miles an hour. Everything's out of your way. Keep it if you can." His tone implied that it would be a miracle if I could. Just then Mr. Halstead walked past the engine and said in a gruff voice, without looking at me, "I want to run forty miles an hour."

That was simple—I let her out to forty. Although we had no indicator in the cab in those days, any engineer who was worth his salt could tell to the second how fast he was running. But we had scarcely reached Chenango Fork when the air-whistle blew to slow down, and again the other side of Norwich. I was getting anxious. We would never make the schedule, if we kept on losing time. But after we left Hubbardsville, the whistle signalled to speed up, and we bumped through the swamp over the worst stretch of track on the road at more than forty miles. If that was the way he wanted to ride, why should I care? At Richfield Springs the old fellow strode by the engine with a smile on his face, but he never looked up or said a word. Not long afterward he had the roadbed repaired.

That was always his way. Neither the first time that I pulled him nor the last, did Mr. Halstead ever thank me or say that I had made a nice run. A few weeks after the blow fell, I pulled Mr. Truesdale, the new President and General Manager, over the road in the same car for an inspection trip. Curiously I watched him talking to Dan beside the steps. He had come from the Rock Island road, they said, and he was a fine, tall, kindly gentleman who was not afraid to smile. He was asking Dan what terminal he ran out of and if the crew followed him around. Scarcely believing the evidence of my ears, I heard him tell Dan to pull in at Greene, where we would all have dinner. My sainted grandmother, the man was actually thinking that we might be hungry!

When we took the siding and the porter came front to invite the fireman and me to dinner in the private car, we felt too grubby to eat with the President; so the porter brought us two trays of a marvelous steak dinner with all the fixings. Back at the enginehouse, when we told how we had dined with the new president—naturally we didn't mention the trays in the cab for we *had* been invited—the boys wouldn't believe it.

"Come on," they said, "don't lie. Tell us what he was like."

After the new officers took over, the Old Man was one of the first to go, and it almost broke his heart.

"I don't know how long I'll be here, Joe, the way they're shipping them," he said to me the last time I saw him in Utica. "I'm glad of it. These fellows don't know how to

run a railroad." He took a few hopping steps as if he was trying to dance. "I'm going to lay off."

A big lump rose in my throat, and I wanted to stick out my hand; but I knew that if I showed him how sorry I felt, he would knock my block off. Old Tom didn't live more than six months after he left the yard, and every one of us missed him around the enginehouse. There was something magnificent and fierce about the way he loved the road, and we were always secretly proud of having the roughest, toughest, cussingest Master Mechanic who ever scorched an engineer.

The old employees did not fit so easily into the new order. But among the innovations was a pension system for those who reached seventy years; so many of the men who could, dropped out. Tom's old board with the T pegs was scrapped, along with the train numbers and the big old time-book that Rogers kept. Now we recorded our own time in slip books, tore off the slip and saved the stub. We were to be paid by the mile, and as this new regulation boosted our pay by about a third, it was not hard to take. The men began to blow about the fine new management. No rough stuff now—if anything went wrong, the brass hats would figure it out with you in a nice way and help you, instead of assuming that it was your fault.

Of course there were some new rules that went hard with us. The engines were pooled on the freight runs— they belonged to the road now, instead of to the engineer —and a man couldn't get up much affection for them when he ran a different one every day. And the oil and waste were rationed scientifically. We didn't have all we could steal from the Old Man.

We had efficiency engineers, who explained to us how much oil, for instance, we needed for a mile. The instructor came along to my engine one afternoon as I was going off and asked me how much oil I used a trip. He was a pleasant fellow, not at all dictatorial, so I said about a couple of quarts.

"Then your lubricator nozzle must be open too far," he told me, "and you are getting a lot more than you need." He climbed into the cab and looked at the lubricator which oiled the steam cylinder—a reservoir with a glass tube showing the oil as it dropped through. Tightening the screw that regulated the flow, he adjusted it until the drops fell separate and oval, as if from a medicine dropper. It was a fallacy, he said, to think that the more oil you feed it, the better the engine runs. Then he got his pencil and a little chart, figured the time and distance between Utica and Binghamton and told me that a drop every ten seconds was enough.

"Try it and see if it doesn't work." I did and was fascinated to see that oil could be measured with such exactitude. But some of the older engineers thought it a lot of poppycock.

Not long afterward the new superintendent sent for me, and I went with an inner quaking, wondering if he was going to put the finger on me. Instead he told me that he had been instructed to pick four train employees to attend a two months' course of instruction in Chicago—a course sponsored by the Scranton Correspondence School. Each division was sending a conductor, an engineer, a fireman, and a brakeman (or trainman, as the shacks now called themselves); all expenses were paid and also our regular wages while we were away. The engineer must have had ten years of experience and be under thirty-five years of age, so it seemed that I just fitted.

That very evening we left on a special Pullman—my first ride in a sleeper and first adventure in a dining car. The crews from Syracuse and Buffalo were already aboard, and by the time we picked up the quota from Scranton, we were all in such high spirits that we sounded like a Democratic convention.

In the dining car, while I was making way with half a broiled chicken and fresh strawberries, I felt someone staring at me and looked across the aisle at a man of about my age. He was vaguely familiar, a big sandy fellow with a squint in one eye. Where had I seen that squint? Red, Red Schmidlap. My memory flipped back to the weathered clapboard school; to Uncle Dinny Dunn, the Irish shoe-maker who whaled me when I played hookey; and Bill Clute, the schoolmaster who tried to use the ruler on me for singing a parody on *Old Dog Tray*, and expelled me when I pulled his whiskers. Red was the leader of a gang who called themselves the Scalpers, sons of well-to-do farmers, with nickels, even dimes in their jeans.

When the conductor who belonged to my group finished his strawberries, Red came over, sat down across the nar-row table and asked if I wasn't Joe Bromley who used to live near Oneida. He told me that he had left the farm and taken to the rails, seen the country from one end to the other, riding the tops, until a girl gave him the glad eye, and he settled down in home territory. Now he was in brass buttons, the conductor of a passenger running out of Buffalo.

We ordered another cup of coffee. Red leaned his

elbows on the table and laughed until the pepper and salt danced a highland fling.

"Joe, whatever did you put in those cigarettes?"

After all these years I blushed at the thought of the cigarettes. That catastrophe grew out of my envy of Red and his gang and my longing to go to their weekly meetings, which were devoted to the manly sports. One day Red invited me to join the club and told me that it met every Monday afternoon in the outhouse of the Presbyterian Church—a commodious hideout where on weekdays they were measurably free from discovery. Each week one member brought a package of cigarettes. We divided the package and smoked, feeling very grown-up and daring.

As I was the newest member, it would be several weeks before my turn came around; but all the time I kept torturing my brain to think of some way to supply my cigarettes when the fatal week arrived. Buying a package was such a remote possibility that I ruled it out; my older brothers were struggling hard to get along, and if I got a pair of shoes a year and a hand-me-down coat, I was doing well. No, I would have to get the cigarettes some other way. As my time drew near, I was steeped in the blackest gloom, awaiting my disgrace.

On the Saturday before our final meeting, a peddler came by the farm. I saw him stop his smart red-wheeled buggy in front of the gate and, though I wasn't particularly interested, followed him into the parlor for lack of anything else to do. He was trying to sell mother a diamond ring—about as hopeless a prospect as selling her

London Bridge, but she liked to look at it and did buy a yard of calico. While he talked to her, flashing the ring so the light would fall on it, he smoked, rolling his own cigarettes with a neatness and elegance that filled me with envy. He rolled a square of rice paper around a pencil and stuck it by licking the edge. Into the perfect tube he poured tobacco through a tiny funnel made of another paper, and tamped it down with the pencil.

If he could make cigarettes, so could I. There was no fine white paper to be found, but I cut squares from a piece of unrumpled manila wrapping paper, stuck them with flour paste and filled them with some bitter green tobacco leaves that my brother had hung under the eaves of the shed to cure. When I had made twenty, rolling them neatly on the pencil, I made a package out of a scrap of red Christmas paper. I would tell the boys these were special English cigarettes which some one had sent my brother.

Monday afternoon when we gathered at our meeting place, I produced the cigarettes, and the boys looked at them with admiration. We all lit up, but they tasted awful; and in a few minutes we were seized with such a colic that we were writhing and howling on the floor. Every one of us expected to die. It was hours before we dragged ourselves home, too sick and miserable to care about our punishment. As Red and I laughed about them, those cigarettes seemed absurdly funny, but I hadn't forgotten the prick of my childish humiliation.

Red and I saw a good deal of each other in Chicago, although he was in the operations and rules division, and we engineers and firemen were taking a stiff mechanical course in addition to operations. At the end of the two months, we were sent home trained in the newest practice in railroading, prepared to be missionaries of the new order. Back in the enginehouse the men were more interested in what we had to eat on the diner and what sights we saw in Chicago than they were in the new rules; but on our own runs we put into practice what we had learned.

After two months on the engine I was taken off again and sent to Scranton, together with a conductor and a train dispatcher, for a further course in train rules. We were coached to be instructors, and when we went home, we organized classes to teach the employees the new standard rules that the road planned to adopt as soon as we were ready for them. All winter we held school, going from station to station, wherever it was most convenient for the men.

Yes, the old times were changing fast. There were new, clean bunkhouses at the terminals, where a man could catch an hour or two of sleep or wash the soot off his face without freezing his hands in outdoor faucet water squirted into a coal bucket. Little holes-in-the-wall that sold coffee and doughnuts and hamburgers were beginning to take the place of the free lunches in saloons.

Men were no longer hired at the nod of the Master Mechanic or the yardmaster; they had to fill out application blanks, pass examinations and show service letters from their last job. The service letters were supposed to catch boomers—the new crop of them that lost their jobs when they went out with Debs in '94. The roads were bitter about the strike of the American Railroad Union and wouldn't take the men back; so many a good railroad man hit the boomer's trail, wandering from road to road under one alias after another, trying to beat the blacklist. It wasn't etiquette in those days to address a boomer by name when you met him again after a year or two—he was most likely travelling under a new one.

The A.R.U. strike didn't affect our division; very few of the men went out. But we soon began to get the influx of boomers from the Middle West. A lot of them got around the service letter requirement by buying letters from a Negro named "Sugarfoot" Burns, in Chicago. For five dollars he sold a man the "secret works" of any brotherhood, a travelling card, and receipts for three months' dues. A service letter cost a buck.

The examinations weren't hard for the old-timers and the boomers who knew their stuff; but they liked to grouse about them—especially the boomers—and complain that it took a college education to get a job of heaving coal. They were always telling us about the wisecracks that they wrote in answer to such questions as "What would you do if the engine wouldn't steam?" or "What do you do when you find a dead body on the track?" The "dead body" was the favorite one. Every boomer claimed that he was the author of the famous answer, "Go through his pockets."

The physical examinations were a good innovation. The younger men got used to the idea of playing kindergarten with strands of colored yarn, to prove that they weren't color blind and of submitting to examinations in the inspection car that carried an eye and ear specialist and a travelling office equipped with the latest eye charts and lenses and devices for testing the hearing. But to some of the older engineers, who were afraid to admit even to themselves that their eyes weren't so sharp as they used to be, or that they didn't always hear the first indications of trouble with the engine, this car grew to be a nightmare.

Nor did the old-timers take kindly to the standardization of everything, from the issues of waste per mile to the number of seconds to blow the whistle—so many seconds for the long toot, so many for the short. What was life coming to, they protested, when you couldn't play *Polly Put the Kettle On* as a signal to your wife, at your own home crossing? As the old engines were discarded and the new ones came in, each like every other of its class, they could no longer put blocks of wood in their whistles to give them a distinctive note. But regimentation has never yet defeated human ingenuity. Polly still recognized the toot and knew when to put the kettle on, even when her man drove a different engine every day.

Time was doing away with the romance and flamboyant individualism of the tough old days, when a man thought nothing of running sixteen or eighteen hours, catching a cat nap and staggering, cursing, to the engine for another run—and made up for it with stolen time on the river catching butterfish or snoozing under an apple tree. And the jolly lies about losing time on account of a bunch of cows on the railroad track were outworn. But on the other hand, a railroad man had a much better chance of living to tell about his adventures than he did in the days when we were making legends.

The side-brakes were gone and the vicious pin couplers; the brotherhoods had succeeded in making air brakes compulsory, required by the Interstate Commerce Commission. Every day new safety devices were giving us a better chance to enjoy our new pensions. There was a lot to be said for the new regime—the fair hearings, regular hours and vacations; but we often felt a twinge of regret for the grand, unregenerate era that produced the Old Man.

22. Ghost of the Old Man

B UT THE GOOD NEW DAYS WERE NOT WITH-
out their terrors: secret fears that stalked
the men on the iron and were whispered
in grumbling undertones about the enginehouse. "Spotting" was one of them. It had its hilarious aspects, but it
put the black check against the name of many a good
railroader whose only fault was a soft heart. The spotters
weren't much of a menace to engineers who didn't spend
too much time crooking the elbow; they were after those
minority fellows who glanced stealthily about a saloon
before they ordered a glass of beer and, if they thought
they saw a suspicious customer, said in a loud voice, "Hey,
can you lend me a match?"

When the company called in Moon-eye O'Shaunessey
and confronted him with a snapshot showing him about
to put his mouth to a bootleg of suds, we made a joke
about his protest, "It couldn't possibly be me!" We could
see the company's point of view about the unreliability of
an employee who habitually tanked up in a saloon; but
we were grim and resentful about traps to catch conductors whose records were clear.

The case of Ed Saunders, a conductor of high rating

and a very good friend of ours, haunted Dan and me for days. The spotter who got Ed was a pretty young woman with a couple of little children. She was riding without a ticket, and when Ed tried to collect her fare, she had no money. Looking up at him with tears in her eyes, she said that she had to get to Norwich to take care of her sick mother and that she would surely be at the station to give him the money on his return trip. Ed knew he oughtn't to do it, but he was a soft-hearted fellow and couldn't stand to see a woman cry; so when both of the children set up a howl, he said, "All right, you can go ahead, but don't forget."

The next day Ed was on the carpet, fired, although he didn't have another black mark against his entire record. Dan and I both worried about Ed, but I tried to shake us out of it; for a railroad man must laugh at misfortunes—his own and everybody's—or he'll turn into a grouch, one of those moody old-timers whom nobody wants to draw for a running partner. The next day, before we pulled out of Utica, I beckoned to Dan.

"You see that innocent-looking old hayseed getting on the third coach? He's a spotter." Dan didn't know whether or not to take me seriously. He circled all around the old fellow, obviously a farmer who had never been ten miles from home.

"I think you're mistaken, Joe," he said. "That nice old clodhopper couldn't spot anything." But I insisted.

"I'm telling you, and I know."

Of course the farmer had his ticket, and so, it happened,

did everybody else in the car; but Dan said he would get even with me for a jittery ride.

Ed's bad luck, although it had no connection with the fear that was creeping up on me, came at the right moment to spur me to action. My secret terror was the eye and ear car that came over the line about once a year to examine engineers and firemen. My right ear, the one next the cab window, was becoming slightly deaf; and some day the doctor in that car was going to catch up with me. I was just turned forty, with my two boys to educate. I had reached the top of the ladder in railroad jobs, pulling one of the crack passengers; there was nothing further to hope for. So I began to brood about the day when the Master Mechanic would send for me and say, "Sorry, Joe, tough luck about the ear. I reckon you'd better bid in a switch engine." That would break my heart.

Thinking over all the jobs that would keep me with the railroads, I decided to try for an appointment as Inspector of Safety Appliances with the Bureau of Safety of the Interstate Commerce Commission, a position that was not then under Civil Service. There were only a few appointments for the entire United States, and several applicants ahead of me; but through the influence of my good friends Mr. Woodburn, an ace conductor on the Delaware & Hudson, and Senator Hinman, the most prominent lawyer in the state and an old railroad man, I finally received the appointment.

For twenty-seven years I rode the plush, from Mexico to Maine and from Pennsylvania to California, investigating wrecks, checking equipment and gossiping with home guards and boomers in every state of the Union. Then I came home to settle on the banks of the Chenango, within sight and sound of the engines. I could lie in bed at night and hear the trains go by, listen to the steady growl of the blackbirds dragging coal, the merry rhythm of the fast passengers, the *chug chug, chug,* CHUG (three soft beats and a snort) of a "lame old girl" with the valve stem out of line.

Those were good days, riding the cushions and learning that railroaders in godforsaken little junctions of the Rockies were very much like their drawling, hide-skinned cousins in lower Florida. Whatever their lingo, and whether they called a caboose a crummy, a doghouse, a shanty, or a hearse (as they do in Pennsylvania), they were everywhere the same daft brotherhood, bewitched by the music of iron wheels. But for me the overstuffed ease of the observation car never had the glamor of the hard seat-box on the right-hand side of the cab. I missed the flavor of the tough days when I hung out of the window of the engine with the rain or sleet in my face.

On trips to Utica, once or twice a year, I always tried to catch Number 9, being eager to exchange the news with Walter Yeomans, a Utica boy who succeeded Dan. In an empty drawing-room, speaking softly in the hush of coming dawn, we would talk about the children in the farmhouses along the Chenango, whom we had watched growing up from toddlers swinging on the barnyard gate, waving at the choo-choo, to farmers, bankers, conductors, and engineers.

Before night faded it was milking time, and the dairy

cows were standing in the barnyards waiting for the farmers. As the whistle tooted for the highway crossings, the lights came on in the farmhouses, one after another. Number 9 was the farmers' alarm clock—time to get up when the morning train went by. As I stared out into the graying daylight, twenty years dropped away and I was in the cab again, watching the windows to see if they were lighted; and when we passed a dark one, wondering whether the farmer was ill, or maybe his little girl, who usually waved to me on the return trip; or whether perhaps the father had rebelled for just one morning, rolling over to take an extra nap.

I saw the fireman open the door of the firebox to toss in a lump of coal. The rose glow lighted up the sky; the headlight fell sharp and yellow on the high embankments of a cut; the wheels crossing a bridge made a rumble, like the far-off roll of a drum; the sparks flew from the stack, mingling with the steam exhaust in a fountain of diamonds; and in the east the sky was streaked with red and gold. The mists cleared away from the green slopes of the little hills, the fireman's girl waved from the kitchen door of a farmhouse, we coasted down the grade to the canal, rattled through Schuyler Street and across the swinging bridge, spotted our coaches at the station on the dot and backed the engine to the roundhouse. And on this morning, which I had lifted fresh and sharp from my memory, I met the Old Man coming out of his office, thundering "Why in hell don't you turn out the lights?"